Love
YOU

Small Changes to Quiet the Gremlins &
Tame Those Unhealthy Habits,
Behaviors & Addictions

GENA M. ROTAS

MetaFun

Love YOU: Small Changes to Quiet the Gremlins and Tame Those Unhealthy Habits, Behaviors, and Addictions
By Gena Rotas, LICSW, MSW, M.Ed.

MetaFun Publishing
ISBN: 978-0-9844450-1-1

Contact:
Gena M. Rotas
413-626-6528
GenaRotas@gmail.com
www.genarotas.com

Printed in the United States of America

Contents

Disclaimer.. v

Foreword.. vii

Acknowledgments xiii

1. Introduction... 1

2. Are You Talking About Me?....................................... 8

3. Sacrificing Obnoxious Behaviors Encourages Respect .. 12

4. Where Did Your Healthy or Sober Self Go? 18

5. Who Thought You Were the Best? 27

6. Exercise Willingness Rather Than Will Power 36

7. Just Maybe Your Mother Was Wrong 52

8. Would You Sabotage Yourself to Make Her Right? 59

9. Like a GPS in Your Head, Chatter Never Stops 71

10. Trade in Those Familiar Bedroom Slippers 78

11. Invite Yourself to Be Responsible for Your Life............ 84

12. Wiggle Your Toes and Land in Your Body 90

13. Minimize the Shame Icon Running in the Background 97

14. Mind Dialogue: You Are the One Talking in the
    First Place 103

15. Tricks to Pull One Over On Your Own Brain.............. 107

16. Stop Seeking Experts and Start Living Your Life....... 111

17. Pocket Your Own Best Friend...YOU!........................ 117

18. Straight Talk for the Scaffolding Required 121

19. Watch Out for Dirty Glasses on the Nightstand 127

20. The Last Word on Worry 134

21. Become Familiar with Your Own Brain Power........... 140

22. PSSST! Ever Heard About Air Time?........................ 149

23. Sleep, Health, Sobriety and Your Brain 154

24. How to Make Breathing Work for You........................ 161

25. Four Simple Choices for a Healthy Life..................... 168

26. What About Reinforcing Self-Compassion?............... 171

27. Love Your Stunning, Strobe Light, Spiritual Self....... 178

28. Love Your Sunshine Self 181

29. Love Your Signature Self... 183

30. Love Your Sweet Self... 185

31. The ABC's of Love YOU! 189

32. Did You S.T.U.B. Your Toe? 191

Resources to Inspire... 203

About the Author 205

Take Your Next Step with Gena 207

Disclaimer

This book could be hazardous to your unhealthy habits, behaviors, and addictions.

Just so you know: Only about five percent of the people who pick up this little book will actually engage in the practices it takes to love yourself and to become your own best friend.

Life can be easy, effortless, and deliciously possible when you choose to Love YOU and Love Yourself First.

Foreword

"Would you like another?" asked the kind and upbeat waitress.

Sitting in a small French-themed café in Hudson, New York, I shot a look across the table at my friend Kim. We both nodded in excited agreement and looked forward to our second mimosas over Sunday brunch.

We sat and enjoyed crepes, croissants, and fresh fruit dipped in chocolate, and started to discuss our health aspirations. As we shared our interests in week-long backpacking trips on high-altitude mountains, visions of rock climbing, and possibly even well-defined arm muscles, we knew that eating the way we were that morning was likely not the path that would lead to our shared vision of fitness.

As our luxurious brunch disappeared into our bellies, we decided right then and there to start a new lifestyle—one of healthier foods and a higher level of endurance. Rather than call it a diet or exercise regimen, we agreed on "The Fierce Awakening." This new lifestyle consisted of daily weigh-ins and a plan to lose ten pounds in ten weeks, however we saw fit.

We left that café not only feeling a bit tipsy and very full of sweets, but also feeling confident, excited, and hopeful for day one of The Fierce Awakening.

The Awakening started strong. We were committed, alert, and aware of our food and exercise choices. We talked to each other every day about our new recipe discoveries, amazing nights of sleep, newly found energy, and fun ways to integrate weight training and cardio.

We diligently tracked our meals, our activity, and our weight. Sometimes we had good news to report—a pound or two lost after a week! And other times, we gained a pound or stayed the same.

As weeks wore on, I started to recognize patterns in myself. The fierceness I began with started to wane, and I started to cheat, take days off, and give myself treats. On the weeks when I was more stressed out, busier with work, or feeling out of control, my commitment to The Fierce Awakening was immediately compromised. I opted for chocolate, pizza, wine, and fried food. On the weeks when I felt good, clear, and rested, I was able to eat lean proteins, go to the gym, enjoy a bowl of salad, and sleep like a rock.

I wondered, what was getting in the way of my fierceness? The answer to that question was unclear and weighed on my mind as weeks went by and my weigh-ins became more and more depressing.

Luckily, a savior in the form of this book showed up just in time. *Love YOU* quickly showed me that my abandonment of The Fierce Awakening was not only a derailment of my commitment to a plan made in a café, but it was an abandonment of myself and my dreams.

In the book before you, Gena Rotas clearly and simply describes the addictions we live with and nurture every day. Clearly based on extensive experience in group training and her private psychotherapy and coaching practice, she also gives a myriad of options for opting to go a healthier route, a route that is steeped in self-love, compassion, and forgiveness.

While looking at my actions during The Fierce Awakening, Gena's book has shed light on why this plan could never work for me: I was too entrenched in my own addiction to food as my savior to ever honor my interest in reaching better health. Without understanding and compassionately seeing my relationship with food, the vicious connection between stress and unhealthy eating would continue.

Gena outlines her definition of "sober" in the first couple of chapters and for the first time, has taught me that I am someone who has addictions and can be rid of them and be sober by following her advice.

As someone who has written three books on career and business, given two TEDx talks, built a successful consulting firm and won awards for public speaking, I pride myself on being a lifelong learner, and I love to try new things. After reading this book, I've learned there has been a very important piece of the puzzle missing; one that I didn't assign enough importance to. I hadn't been looking at my buried shame, fears, and triggers that lead to self-sabotage.

Even with success in some areas, it's easy to miss signs of sabotage in others. As Gena says, "There is a part of you that sits silent; watching and listening for an opportunity to show up with the intention to divert you from making healthy choices," she warns. "A 'saboteur' willfully destroys.

When you fall off the wagon, your sabotaging self definitely destroys the sober streak you had going."

What I observed over the last several weeks of my new lifestyle plan is that I can quickly and easily sabotage myself if I don't pay attention.

This book is excellent if you have tried, failed, tried again, and feel stuck or lost when it comes to creating a lifestyle of happiness, self-love, and forgiveness. It is possible to release guilt, shame, and addiction, even if it doesn't seem like a reality right now.

Numerous times in my life when attempting to change a habit, mindset, or belief, I would feel like the road was all uphill in a snowstorm, but Gena shows us that it doesn't have to be that way. This journey can be rewarding, uplifting, awakening, and nothing short of life changing if you let it.

I dog-eared and took notes throughout this entire book, as Gena has expertly laid out the steps to loving your sober self. One point I jotted down and have turned into an affirmation is this: "The transformation into loving yourself takes courage, patience, persistence, practice, willingness, faith, perseverance, kindness, friendship, gentleness, and warm, loving care." Reading this sentence out loud shines a light on the importance of this kind of work if we are to truly show up for our lives and be who we were born to be.

Gena reminds us that no matter what your vice is, whether it's alcohol, food, work, TV, drugs, sex, shopping, or something else, this book is the perfect companion to get you started on a healthy track that you can walk on your own, with friends, or in a group. The first place to start is accepting that it's time to change and knowing that it's totally possible to Love YOU.

As for me, I'm doing take-two of The Fierce Awakening. This time I'm trying it actually awakened and totally focused on my sobriety, and loving every part of myself on this journey to discovering, and fully loving, my compassionate, sensitive, and creative self.

To the journey,

Angela Lussier

May 23, 2016

Holyoke, Massachusetts

Acknowledgments

Heartfelt words of thanks to all those who helped cheer me on as I completed this powerful little book. In 2010, I spent time training with Alan Marlott, Sarah Bowen, Neha Chawla, and Joel Grow in the Mindfulness Based Relapse Prevention Program. As I witnessed the team offer unconditional love for the human struggle towards sobriety, I was inspired to widen the field and include all those unhealthy habits, behaviors, and addictions that keep us from experiencing joy in our lives. Originally the title of this book followed as a sequel to the one I wrote called *Love Your Slim Self,* and my intention was to title this book *Love Your Sober Self.* But my passion to reach a greater audience brought about the new idea of simply loving yourself first, and I titled this book *Love YOU: Small Changes to Quiet the Gremlins and Tame Those Unhealthy Habits, Behaviors, and Addictions.*

One reviewer of the manuscript commented that there were just too many ideas throughout the pages of Love YOU. The concern was that people would be overwhelmed with the amount of skills, tools, and strategies. The question raised was "What really was the takeaway?" Thank you for that profound question because it validates the underlying truth and message I want to put forth. The only takeaway from this book is that loving yourself, all of you, unconditionally, is the most precious idea you could incorporate into your life. This book gives you a roadmap to do just that. Love who you are first, and life will become joyous.

With profound and genuine acknowledgment for dear friends and colleagues, thank you for the inspiration and the encouragement to keep on keeping on: Tim and Liz Frangioso, Eric and Rachael Letendre, Donna Hobart and her brother, Donna Sroka, Roy Dudley, Jenny Sharma, Kathleen Conley, Christine Leary, Michael Youmans, Karen Amato, and my long-time friend, Joyce Singer.

Thanks to the folks who helped polish the beginning writings and the final editing: Lizzy Mitchell Kelly, Janice Beetle, and of course, Claudia Gere for her amazing skills in order to help me launch this baby.

Beth Notwick reviewed the manuscript with delicious notes and a warm celebration, while Angela Lussier gave me her personal vote of support and wise review by writing the foreword. Dana Miccuci sealed my commitment to help people be happy with a beautiful spirited endorsement. There is such wisdom in knowing that truly, love does run the show!

With gratitude and appreciation to my daughter Kristin Rotas and her husband, David Axelrad, for their help in making the message easy to comprehend, and my daughter Rachael Jacobs for her joyous encouragement to stay the course in order to follow my heart. My children have always been in my corner, and I am grateful for their feedback, support, inspiration, and love.

Throughout the process of creating this work, my intention has been to witness and validate what it takes to live a healthy life and to hold sobriety as a precious gift. I want to acknowledge all the encouragement, the inspiration, the sharing, the vulnerability, the healing, the wisdom, the courage, the tenacity, the perseverance, the bravery, the creativity, the lightness of heart, and the practice of self-forgiveness of all the people and clients I have had the privilege of working with over the years. I will always treasure your contributions. Most of all, I want to acknowledge the inner intelligence of the heart that is in all of us to remember our own preciousness and that we truly are loved ...unconditionally!

Chapter 1

Introduction

In the fall of 2012, my husband was diagnosed with terminal stage IV cancer. Initially the doctors could not find the origin, and they gave him a prognosis of four months. The shock and hysteria that overtook my personal well-being was turbulent and relentless. My husband, on the other hand, seemed to take the news as a wake-up call to "get all his affairs in order." I thought he was in total denial of what was happening to him and us, but I was wrong. He enthusiastically said, "I have had a great life, and although I don't want to die, I am grateful for all that I have had and do have now."

There was not a fearful bone in his body, and he embraced the cancer with a determined spirit to fight with everything he had. Together we danced a fearless tango during the chemotherapy. Not literally, but it was my way of coping with the challenges of treatment. Endless visits to the doctors felt like a tedious and monotonous foxtrot; a hilarious Charleston when good news and possible remission graced the CAT scans. Then finally a loving and delicate waltz when the cancer returned.

My husband lived for two more years after that initial diagnosis, and he embraced every living minute of his time here on the planet. Whenever he would call on the phone or leave a voice mail, he would close the conversation with the words: "Love you!"

It is not by accident that his affectionate words have become the title of this book. Perhaps it is by a design greater than I will ever know.

I have kept a recording of his voice mails and it gives me a smile when I listen to the recording of his voice. "Sweeeeetheart," he would call me, and when he said good-bye, he would end with "love you!" I knew then and know now that each time he said "love you," he was reaching out to connect with a heartfelt sense of love and appreciation.

I have taken his salutation and refocused the lens to place it on the love you can have for yourself. Love YOU means to love you, that real you; the you that you are meant to be. Love the authentic you, even if you are not sure who that you is. Loving yourself comes first and unless you do fall in love with yourself, life continues to be a struggle. *Love YOU* is meant to help you come to love who you are in order to come to know what you want. This book will help you make the small changes to get you to that place.

Might I suggest that you begin using the word love, especially if that has not been part of your everyday vocabulary? You can start by telling people you care about that you love them just for being your friend, or for being so special, or just for being who they are. When you say goodbye to someone you do love, add "love you" to the close. It might be the last words you speak, or the last words they hear.

Initially the title of this book was *Love Your Sober Self*. In my work, I spent many years counseling people struggling with addictions, and I wanted to offer them a new way to achieve sobriety. After much soul-searching and talking with others, it was clear that addictions are only a part of the complicated struggle many of us encounter as human beings. We battle with a variety of unhealthy habits and ugly behaviors which compromise our intentions to be present, available, compassionate, loving, and productive in our lives.

Most of us are in a tug-of-war with the inner critic of our personal inventory. Those voices that shout damaging statements and create dusty thinking prevent us from feeling whole, vibrant, confident, and loved. We all have that default in our thinking; gremlins, I call the voices, and it is time to quiet their harsh tactics which squelch our brilliance.

Some of us are unaware of the power that abrasive murmurings have on our self-esteem and our self-worth. When we simply concede to the expressions of criticism, doubt, rejection, suspicion, indecisiveness, reservation, and mistrust, we often are responding from a very deep place of past experience; and it feels familiar, but not friendly and not good.

All that negative internal dialogue coming from those robust gremlins can lead to self-hatred and self-loathing.

Often the sense of familiarity is safer and easier to tolerate because we have been there before and each time we return to self-hatred, we reinforce the power of that illogical thinking. Self-hatred is a huge backpack we invisibly hold behind our consciousness. It is filled with the damaging messages and events usually from our early years as children. It continually gets heavier throughout our lives when we encounter situations that bring up the messages we believed as children. When we forget to empty the contents of our internal self-talk, the weight of doubt prevents us from loving ourselves, which in and of itself will magically lighten the load.

Lightening the load and walking through your life with an ease and a step of delight is an aspiration worth considering. Just imagine how it would feel to say truly, "I am a happy camper," and "Life is *good!*"

Who would say that anyway? Would you ever consider thinking such thoughts: "Life is easy and effortless." "Life is good and I am worthy of happiness." "I am confident and positive about my abilities." "It is easy for me to make healthy and life-affirming decisions for my well-being." "I deserve to have the best life has to offer." And all of those other positive, self-affirming statements that give you confidence and make you feel worthy.

Instead we often struggle with an inner voice of critical and judgmental comments. Those internal gremlins have their script memorized, and at lightning speed they fill our heads and our souls with a dialogue of guilt, shame, embarrassment, and self-disgust.

Taming those voices is first an act of loving the part of you that notices they are talking. By noticing what you are saying to yourself, you can begin to edit the inner talk. Throughout this little book, you will be introduced to ideas that will guide you through skills and strategies to quiet the voices in your head and rewrite the self-talk which will support your health and well-being. After all, you are in charge, and it is time to take back your power.

The bottom line: love *you* no matter what!

This is the first how-to book you will ever read that starts out by telling you to stop trying.

First, you need to understand this book is not about *changing you*. It's about learning to *love you*, the you that has always been there, and will support your journey towards the idea of thriving and flourishing in your life.

Being at ease and healthy comes when you love yourself first.

Today is the last time you'll ever need to reflect on all the times you have tried to change unhealthy habits or raging addictions. It is not about the broken promises you made to yourself to stop destructive behaviors only to find yourself engaged in the cycle of self-hate and discouragement.

Every plan, strategy, or program in the past has failed you—you did not fail them. They emphasized just what you want to avoid: that awful teeth-gritting, hand-clenching element called willpower, which isn't power at all, because "willing" is all about trying too hard, and trying is pointless. Yoda, the character in *Star Wars: The Empire Strikes Back,* is an inspiration. He told Luke Skywalker that there is "No try," there is just "Do, or do not."

With all your past efforts, your focus has been just a little off, like a camera that is aimed to the right of your shoulder instead of on you. Your focus is now on you, the entire you, and I want you to know that making healthy choices and thinking of it as being sober, is the part of you that you have neglected to love.

After years of always trying much too hard, there is a way for you to experience the process of being authentic and natural in a comfortable and easy way and through a process that is guaranteed to transform your life.

Love YOU is about a change in feelings. It is not about all the programs in the past that have failed you. It is not about rigid behaviors and deprivation. It is not about physical, emotional, and psychological exhaustion.

There is an unspoken myth that if you really want success, you have to fight for it. You have to give up the pleasures of life, be denied, be deprived, and struggle for success. What if I told you that just isn't true?

In *Love YOU* there is an acknowledgement that in the past you have tried too hard; much too hard! There is an uncomplicated way to successfully be healthy and to ensure a fulfilling and wholesome lifetime of success.

Give yourself permission to consider the ideas in this little book. Acknowledge that you picked up this book because something caught your eye or your heart. Maybe now, as you read this, you may even find yourself thinking...

- How do I love me?

- Why would I want to love me?

- If I am already healthy why do I have to love myself?

- When I slip and find myself in my unhealthy habits or addictive behaviors, how could loving myself make a difference?

- I already hate myself, how could I ever find love for me?

- What the heck is a "real authentic self?"

- What does love have to do with being happy or healthy?

...and on and on as your mind tries to make sense out of this amazing idea that loving yourself can change your life.

Chapter 2
Are You Talking About Me?

Perhaps you are laughing at the idea of even imagining a "real self." Could you be asking yourself right now, "How could I even think of myself as real or authentic when I have been struggling with unhealthy habits, behaviors, and addictions of one kind or another?" At this point in your life, you might be spending time working hard to cover those habits up, or better yet, just denying that those unhealthy behaviors actually exist.

If so, consider this age-old proverb that warns for caution:

"Curiosity killed the cat and satisfaction brought it back."

Originally the quote referred to care or worry. Care and worry killed the cat, but satisfaction brought it back. Are you worried about yourself, even a little bit? Maybe you do care about what choices you have been making and would like to consider changing, but not too drastically, and with not much effort.

Cats are certainly curious, inquisitive risk-takers. The satisfaction of knowing what makes something so interesting and being able to understand and explain it, whether to a cat or not, keeps us coming back for more.

What if you were willing to simply be curious about your life? Consider the intuitive act of wanting to know about how to make life easier and even effortless. Perhaps you might have a thirst for such valuable wisdom without needing to spend excessive time or money. You could unlock the key to having your life run smoothly, with less stress and with less drama.

This is the first time I have mentioned "stress and drama" and I would like to bring your attention to a reality that most of us might agree on. With all the expectations of personal aspirations, family life, working environments, professional commitments, community involvement, hectic schedules, compromised health issues, and countless other pressures, we are sometimes collectively living a life that might feel like it is Scotch® taped together; one little extra push or pull and it will all fall apart. Can you relate? Have you ever felt so stressed out that just one more thing that doesn't go your way will take you down?

Could this be you, when you are so stressed out that you....

♦ Eat most of the Halloween candy the kids brought home

♦ Finish off the half gallon of ice cream before dinner

♦ Buy two bags of chips; one for the ride home, and the other for later

- Yell at your kids, partner, friend, cat, dog, or bird for no good reason
- Start a fight with your kids, family, partner, or co-worker
- Max out your credit card
- Bite your nails to the quick
- Engage in road rage
- Get a migraine
- Take extra pills
- Waste time on Facebook
- Surf the web for hours
- Drive too fast and get a speeding ticket
- Miss your exit
- Drink too much
- Eat too much
- Smoke too much
- Pick up drugs
- Stay out too late
- Not go to work
- Not eat
- Spend too long at the gym
- Forget

Pressures, tensions, disappointments, defeats, let-downs, frustrations, overwhelm, traumas, and life's little miserable moments can take you to the place where unhealthy habits, behaviors, and addictions automatically take over. Choosing to engage in unhealthy behavior can possibly give you some relief by anesthetizing your feelings and emotions, or by giving you something familiar to do while you wait for the pain to pass.

If you are willing to be curious, like the cat, I promise that you will come to a solid place of understanding and, with satisfaction, find ways to bring you and your life back into healthy balance. Believe it or not, you already have everything you need and all of the resources within you. *Love YOU* will show you how to soak in the good so you can orchestrate a thriving life for the rest of your days.

Chapter 3

Sacrificing Obnoxious Behaviors Encourages Respect

Have you ever felt that your habits and addictions have been running your life and could be dangerous to your happiness? You may be tired, lonely, depleted, exhausted, and frustrated, and you probably want some answers that bring relief.

Give yourself permission to use that care and curiosity we talked about in the first chapter to lay your unhealthy habits and addictive behaviors to rest, not kill them. For some of us, our addictive behaviors have become friends we can rely on. Depending on the severity of the addiction, it comes with an army of other behaviors that keep us from living a healthy lifestyle.

Shirley looked forward to her nightly routine of eating a dish of ice cream while watching her favorite TV show just before bed. The kids were asleep, her husband was snoring at the other end of the couch, and she could heap in as much of the frosty dessert as she wanted.

No one was there to tell her to stop, only the threat of diabetes and her skyrocketing weight. She was feel-

ing apprehensive and worried about her annual physical in the upcoming month. Occasionally her anxiety would creep into her ice cream bowl, and she would go back for seconds. The habit of eating more ice cream than she wanted or needed had become a familiar routine or behavior. She felt shame, guilt, and disgust while she brushed her teeth before bed. She couldn't even make herself imagine what she would do if she had to give up her nightly comfort activity.

Let's set the stage for further discussion of habits and addictions, which encompass a myriad of behaviors. Addictions can often be lingering in the background of your thinking, just waiting for that opportunity to catch you off guard. You might have an unhealthy addiction to drugs, alcohol, gambling, or food, and you are already on a supportive journey to help yourself stay sober. This book will help you to develop, and then underscore, the encouraging self-compassion which is vital to staying the path of healthy sobriety.

The latest research tells us that when we slip or engage in unhealthy behaviors or addictions, the earlier we practice self-forgiveness and are willing to support ourselves with compassion, the sooner we can get back on track and begin anew.

Being sober might sound like it's not for you because you are not dealing with the heavy-duty addictions that require vigilant awareness and supportive connection to choose healthy rather than damaging behaviors.

For me, turning a challenging concept or idea into an acronym helps broaden the meaning of the initial word. You will find this a number of times throughout this little book. This is why I have decided to use the word SOBER to mean:

S...Sacrificing

O...Obnoxious

B...Behaviors

E...Encourages

R...Respect

Let's begin with the end of the SOBER acronym:

R = Respect

To truly respect ourselves for who we are takes courage. Struggling to reconcile our personal shortcoming begins with us feeling a sense of wonder and awe of our own precious magnificence. To have reverence, admiration, and positive regard for ourselves is an ongoing process. We are always truly a work in progress.

E = Encourages

Encouraging ourselves to be hopeful and helpful creates a positive outlook on changing for the better. Rather than look for perfection, because perfection is usually a pressure cooker idea, instead encourage ourselves to be better in the present moment than we were in the moment before; to make things better, not perfect.

B = Behaviors

Refers to all the habits, actions, addictions, personal traits, manners, activities, tricks, conduct, offenses, aggressions, discourtesies, doings in our lives that we would like to change, tame, subdue, alter, modify, and tone down.

O = Obnoxious

If the behaviors we would like to change were anything other than obnoxious, they would be loving, and we would be totally enamored with ourselves.

S = Sacrificing

Sometimes the word sacrifice can mean to just "give up" something. Like I am going to make a sacrifice and give up chocolate for a week. (Ugh, not!)

When we can sacrifice the obnoxious behaviors in our lives, we have the freedom to consider respecting ourselves from a new and wholesome vantage point.

Use your genuine curiosity and investigate satisfying information to support your efforts to live a fulfilling life. Integrate and practice the ideas and exercises in this book and you will find an easy, healthy, and lasting way to live, which promises freedom, happiness, inner peace, and abundant joy.

As a way to integrate health, wellness, emotional balance, resilience, strength, and good decision-making, I will use the words "sober" and "sobriety" to mean healthy, wholesome, sensible, reasonable, and good for you. I realize that being sober gives the idea of being free from addictive drugs and alcohol, but being sober, calm, and serious, truly means making healthy choices, which equals fewer problems in any area of your life.

Let yourself exchange the ideas of sobriety and health throughout this book and give yourself permission to think of a healthy life as a sober one.

Repetition and practice are the magic ingredients for what it takes to Love YOU. You might have been repeating and practicing counterproductive behaviors and addictive habits up until this point, and you might be willing to consider small, gentle changes that will catapult you towards an easier way of living. You will find ideas, skills, strategies, and suggestions repeated a number of times, sometimes in a new frame or from a different point of view. For example, reminding yourself to take a deep breath is a skill, and my recommendation that offers you an opportunity to slow down, reflect on what is happening, and have enough oxygen traveling to your brain to help you make a decision that is informed, conscious, and intentional for your success. If you do nothing else while reading this book, remember to keep breathing!

Throughout the book, you will encounter a variety of personal stories, which will give you a clearer sense of the real-life struggles, challenges, and successes others have experienced. The names and identities of those who have so generously contributed to this writing have been changed and their accounts are testimony to our connection to each other and the healing of the human spirit.

You will also find contributions and reflections from individuals who want you to know that their thinking and life wisdom has made a difference for them. My heartfelt appreciation and gratitude for all the charitable contributions they have passed along so that you might consider positive action towards yourself in your quest to Love YOU.

Chapter 4

Where Did Your Healthy or Sober Self Go?

You have always had the "other side" of life available to you. That is, the "healthy side," or as we are defining it, the "sober side" of life, where health and wellness are everyday events. Your sober self has loved you with unconditional acceptance and positive regard no matter what unhealthy behaviors have shown up. The healthy part of you or your sober self is quietly waiting for you to make a different choice.

Don't go looking for your sober self during a self-defeating binge on food, drugs, or alcohol. You won't find your sober self during a heavy morning hangover. Your healthy self is not hiding in that empty pill bottle or with the last puff of smoke. You won't find your sober self after working a ninety-hour week or lingering on the last scratch ticket in your pocket.

Your healthy self, your sober self, is not visible when you say goodbye to the fifteenth sweetheart in a month or at the drive-in while you wolf down yet another dozen do-nuts. Your healthy self waits patiently while you search the internet for sex and while you dance with rage and anger

over those behaviors over which you seem to have no control. Whether you are suffering with addictions to M&M'S®,
jelly beans, cleaning, performance, perfection, cell phones,
texting, Facebook, computers, sugar, eating, gambling, unhealthy relationships, anger, rage, work, sex, alcohol or
drugs, *Love YOU* will put you on the fast track to health,
well-being, sobriety, and contentment…aka happiness!

Let's ask the question one more time: Where did your
healthy or sober self go? There is a place inside of you that
remembers. We all came into this world sober, and for most
of us, in a state of healthy bliss.

As an infant you had only one responsibility: to keep
breathing. The medical team went to work weighing and
measuring, prodding and poking, cleaning and swaddling,
in order to make sure you were ready for your entry into the
world beyond the womb.

Your conception itself is a mathematical miracle. Out of
the billions of people on the planet, the only two who could
have made you somehow managed to find each other. Then,
the only pairing among the millions of sperm and eggs
somehow resulted in a pregnancy. Consider the mathematical odds of being conceived, and you'll find a much better
chance of winning your state lottery.

As if conception weren't challenging enough, your birth
was a heroic transition. You traveled down your mother's
birth canal, and the trauma associated with the birthing
process lingers in your very cells. It doesn't matter if you
were an emergency birth or a Cesarean section. You moved

between life and death and briefly gave up oxygen from the umbilical cord to welcome the breath of life into your lungs. Then as a newborn, you started breathing and began your life journey.

Perhaps at this point in your life you are struggling to return to that natural state of well-being. You might be exhausted from the unhealthy and addictive behaviors that have tampered with your desire to be healthy. No matter what they are, your addictions have kept you in a state of perpetual confusion, and (if they are severe enough) walking the line between life and death while you figure out how to make healthy choices and stay sober.

There is something unique about calling for help at the end of an addictive binge. When you have broken the bank, have no one to turn to; when you are scared, sick, desperate; that is when you call for help, usually at the end of a destructive binge.

Do we call for help because we are scared, frightened, and desperate at the idea of being without the addictive behaviors and not knowing what to do next? Or do we call for help because there is a part of us reluctant to give up the idea that recovery is possible?

The wisdom within these pages will help you welcome the healthy choices of living fully in this world and support you in letting go of and giving up the insanity of existing through behaviors that cause you heartache and pain, isolation and despair.

Infants are pure joy. You were an infant once, innocent and waiting...to be loved and cherished, encouraged and validated, honored and supported, cared for and nurtured, nourished and guided to find purpose and meaning to your life. Perhaps it is only a matter of remembering that indeed you are on that quest for pure joy. Remembering is a lifetime journey. Take a moment and go find this video online.

Baby's First Bath by ElepnantJournal.co:

http://www.elephantjournal.com/2012/04/skip-your-morning-meditation-watch-this-instead/

The infant in the video surrenders to love, life, and acceptance of her own magnificence and perfection. She is bathed with a sense of ease and connection to her caretaker. The water is soothing, warm, and delicious, similar to the fluid in her mother's womb from which she emerged. You were that infant once, and loving yourself is a beginning for change and healing. Relaxing into love is a ticket to joy, peace, and ease in life.

Asking the question, "Where did your sober self go?" implies that there was a separation; that you are missing a part of yourself. The truth is that you were never separate from your sober self, your healthy self, your lovely self, your precious self, or from any other part of you, for that matter. Your sober, healthy self has always been an essential part of your very essence. You were born sober and even though you might have been through or still are experiencing some very difficult addictive struggles, your sober self has been waiting to simply reconnect and inspire you to orchestrate healthy choices in order to flourish in life.

Henry's story is more common than we would like to think. You might know someone who packed away the possibility of living fully and enjoying life again. While Henry didn't experience the result of living an unfulfilling life overnight, his disconnection with those who love him started with his failing to love himself.

Henry found the entire idea of "loving himself" rather impossible. It was very clear to him that he, in fact, "hated himself." Family life was stressful, chaotic, and no longer any fun. His three teenage children were demanding and irritating, his wife was aloof and distant, and his coworkers had begun excluding him from their social events.

After work he would stop by his favorite pub for a couple of beers and saunter home, often too late for supper. An extra plate was usually on the stove waiting for him and he would wolf down the food with a couple of glasses of wine. Television was a perfect escape to avoid having conversation or arguments with the family. He didn't mind not talking to the kids; they only wanted him to come to their games, watch them play their instruments, and give them money to go shopping. The weeknights were predictable and felt almost numbing. After falling asleep on the couch, he would find his way to bed, usually after midnight, and be up again at 6:00 a.m.

to start the routine all over again.

He used to be glad to come home after work and loved to play with the kids before dinner. There was a time when he and his wife went out at least once a week to enjoy dinner together and maybe even some dancing. Life had changed...or had he changed? Falling in love with himself was the furthest thing from his mind. And why would he want to do that anyway?

Michael has been entertaining the ideas held in these pages and comments about his understanding of the many parts of himself that want stage presence. His authentic self is the part of him that wants health and well-being.

"I have been sober for almost three years, but sometimes even finding my healthy self, my sober self is a challenge. I know that he lives inside me, and he has a very real voice, but he competes for airtime with my many other selves. When I am hungry, angry, lonely, or tired, I hear from my 'resentful self' that feels so darn entitled to that slice of cake because he worked hard today, or my 'victim self, perfectionist self' who is feeling so put out because despite all of his hard work keeping himself sober, his personal relationships are not yet where he wants them....

"Amidst all my kooky selves, I find my sober self—or my authentic self—the one who provides me with the wisdom, patience, and resolve to breathe, pause, and make a good decision.

"Oftentimes, I refer to my many selves as my Committee. I go through life with companions: my many selves; but my healthy self, my sober self. has to run the show. I am the Chairman of the Committee."

While your addictions, self-defeating behaviors, or habits that get in the way of a healthy, fulfilling life may not have reached the point illustrated by Michael's story, you can avoid that path by focusing now on the beginning steps for Loving YOU.

Love Your Significant Self

Seven Ways to Begin Falling in Love with You

When you were a kid and learning how to manage the rules of life, the grown-ups around you were the ones who reminded you to do what was important. Parents reminded you to brush your teeth twice a day. Grown-ups reminded you to look both ways when you crossed the street. Teachers reminded you to do your homework, and relatives reminded you to mind your manners.

Now that you are a grown-up and the most significant person in your life is you, you still need some reminders. Here is a list of seven reminders that will get you started on the path to Loving YOU:

1. Tell yourself that you are in the process of "falling in love" with yourself and that your health and well-being are now a priority.

2. You don't have to believe that you Love YOU just yet. Just choose to entertain the thought.

3. Write on a card and post it in your world:

   ♦ "I get to ask for what I want."

   ♦ "I get to make my own choices."

   ♦ "I get to keep learning."

   ♦ "I get to love *me*!"

4. Frame a picture of yourself when you were happy, smiling, and in love with life. It might be a picture of when you were younger or even a precious baby picture.

5. Post a picture of yourself on your mirror. Each time you see it, say: "Hello there, lovely self. I do deserve to have a healthy, happy, sober life."

6. Each morning, speak your messages out loud to yourself. Your voice reflects the beliefs you hold within. Tell yourself each morning your intentions for the day and let no one deter you from your personal design for change.

7. Muster up enthusiasm, excitement, commitment, and conviction in your voice.

Use a mirror and look directly into your own eyes and say out loud:

♦ Today I choose to be sober.

- Today I choose to be happy.

- Today is amazing; I get another chance to keep breathing.

- No one can stop me, not even myself.

- I am ready, willing, and excited about today.

- Today is the first day of the rest of my life.

- I simply love *you*.

Take a moment to reflect on your own glorious preciousness. You came into this world as a beautiful and complete being held in unconditional love for who you are. Find a quiet place within yourself and consider the thought that you can find that truth again. Regardless of what your decisions have been in the past, each new day, each new breath, gives you another chance to think differently about yourself.

If you have already reached the point where you no longer feel connected to those around you, trust that those around you are always connected, you just don't realize it yet. Be willing to engage fully in living a life you want. See a possible path opening in front of you and practice these seven simple ways to begin the process of Loving YOU. The next chapter will help you learn about the impact you've made on someone in your life who thought you were the best, even before you believed that for yourself.

Chapter 5

Who Thought You Were the Best?

Every child deserves at least one adult in their life who is crazy about them. Perhaps there is someone you can remember from your youth who thought you were just the best. It might have been a parent, a neighbor, a teacher, a relative, a coach, or a family friend.

Try to recall someone in your life who helped you feel important and special. Take a moment to focus your thoughts on that person. When you think of them, you might remember a story about being with them and listening to what they told you about yourself. You knew that they loved you unconditionally and would always be there for you when times were tough.

That individual encouraged you, supported you emotionally, and sometimes might have even comforted you physically. They had such faith in you and thought you were amazing. They helped you feel like a million bucks and you adored telling them about your successes and were never afraid to tell them about your struggles.

If you have gotten this far, if you are reading this book and you can't remember anyone who loved you this way, then there was a very special part of you that carried the responsibility of loving yourself so dearly. You knew you were special, and you had a very deep and profound faith and understanding that you would always be OK. You can thank the part of you that knows you are precious. Capture that feeling, whether it is you alone or with that special someone who loved you.

What you think about certainly has an impact on your behavior. Let's create a metaphor for how you think and what those thoughts might mean for you.

Have you ever stopped long enough to watch the wind? You might notice the wind while you are taking a walk, sitting on your porch, or riding along on your bicycle. You could see a gust of wind, a balmy breeze, a playful wind among the wildflowers or a rustling wind in the branches of the trees, or clouds swirling at sunset. You might have experienced times when you were in the midst of a hurricane wind or even a tornado, some of which could have been destructive and devastating. The truth is there is nothing you can do to change the wind, slow it down, or even make the wind go faster. You might be able to harness the wind for its energy, but you cannot actually stop the wind. Rather than see the wind, you can witness the changes that take place when it passes by.

What if you considered your thoughts as just "wind in your brain"? If thoughts are like the wind, then you understand that you really can't control all your thinking. Thoughts fly in and out like the wind. Memories do the same thing. Often you can't remember the last thought you had before you began thinking about that childhood game of dodgeball or digging for worms to go fishing.

When a painful memory shows up without warning, your entire body could go into overload. Because the mind does not know the difference between what is real and what is imagined, your body thinks it is happening all over again. The trigger could be a smell, a taste, an image, or a picture. Someone might share a memory of his or her own and instantly your brain chimes in with a similar event from your past.

Biologically we are wired for survival, and when we feel threatened or in danger, our brains stimulate the stress response that causes a cascade of physical symptoms. Your body might begin to sweat; your stomach could flip and feel sick, your heart might start to pound, and your thinking could seem foggy. That's when windy thoughts are painful and bring up trauma from the past.

Mustering up the courage to recall the positive memories of being loved by someone in your past takes courage, compassion, conscious choice, determination, and practice. What did you feel when you allowed yourself the luxury of remembering that you were loved? Sit for a minute with the physical expression in your body. Perhaps you might notice a warmth around your heart, a smile on your face, a calmness to your breathing, and a yearning for that person to show up again.

They can, they are, they will—the love they displayed for you is always available. Remember that the mind doesn't know what is real or what is imagined. When you imagine their caring for you, it is real and you can use it as harnessed "wind in your brain."

For a variety of reasons, our motivation to remember the negative usually takes center stage. Realizing that the negative thoughts are quicker to show up is pivotal to creating change and movement towards loving yourself. You can't blame your "windy brain" for all the problems in your life. Sorry, it just doesn't work like that!

The good news is that you can have an impact on your thinking. Unlike the wind, which you cannot control, you do have the ability to choose your thoughts. When you are ready to accept responsibility for the thoughts you choose to think, you are learning how to harness that "wind in your brain" towards a healthy, happy life.

Start by simply watching what passes through your mind. Are the thoughts you are thinking supporting your well-being, or do they cause distress? By remembering to Love YOU, your new thinking moves you toward making healthy and positive choices.

With Healthy Choices, You Have Fewer Problems

Everything is a choice, and we are responsible for the choices we make. The problem is that we never give ourselves time or space to try and decide what it is we really want, and most of the choices are knee-jerk reactions to a stimulus. When we are more aware of the ability to label and choose a response, we are more in charge of our destiny. We choose: positive or negative. It is always our choice.

What would unhealthy and addictive thinking look like? Why would anyone want to use negative thinking as a habit? You can't give up thinking, can you?

Julie's story begins with a realization that life was just not working for her, and her desire to change "something" became her motivation to seek help.

Julie's struggle with her inner dialogue had become a major focus in her life. She grew up in a family of six children with parents who were quick to point out everything she was doing wrong. As the first-born daughter, with four brothers and a baby sister, Julie was the one to fight through life's curveballs. Her father was an active alcoholic, and her mother suffered from episodes of major depression.

Now, at thirty-five years old, Julie filled her life with managing her own family, running the PTA at school, coaching her daughter's soccer team, singing in the choir at church, and working as an emergency room nurse in the nearby hospital.

In her mind, nothing was ever good enough, and Julie spent most of her time criticizing herself for what she felt were her shortcomings. She was constantly on the go, and would fill her time with chores and commitments, searching for approval from others. She felt empty most of the time, like a robot living a life she didn't really want. Her thinking was always "half-empty," and she was beginning to dump her insecurities onto the people she loved the most. Her negative thinking became so habitual that you could consider it an addiction, so as time went on, she hated herself more and more.

The wind in Julie's brain was reaching hurricane proportions, and destruction in the wake of her mental storm was calling for federal aid. Short of a total "mental-ectomy," Julie was willing to begin rewriting the script of thoughts and take charge of the gale force winds of negative thinking. The process of change began with a simple exercise of listing things she was grateful for.... Every night she made a list of ten things she was grateful for during the day and every morning she would read the list. No matter how negative she felt, she persevered writing her list daily, and after a few weeks, there came the calm in the eye of her windy storm. For the first time in years, she felt a sense of hope and relief that her emptiness was beginning to respond to gratitude.

Love Your Smart Self

Seven Ways to Reinforce Your Brilliance

What you think about most of the time is what you get. It really is a simple concept and has very profound consequences. The mind works in words, which create images, which then cause feelings, which are the motivation for our actions.

If words are so powerful, then let's use the word SMART! According to Webster's unabridged dictionary, smart means "exhibiting social ability or cleverness, intellectual knowledge, such as found in books." It can also mean "good looking" as in a smart outfit, or even cleverly humorous as in a "smart remark." The synonyms are: bright, capable, sophisticated, witty, cultivated, educated, learned, attractive, chic, stylish, and handsome.

When you consider loving your smart self, you get to toot your own horn. I don't mean you have to literally shout it from the rooftops, but you have to begin shouting it inside your own head.

I like using the word "smart," because it adds the additional level of competence and image. You are smart in more ways than just your grades in school. And even if you didn't make such good grades, or struggled in the educational system, you are smart because of your life experience and life knowledge, and you are entitled to have the positives working for you.

The antonyms of smart (you remember, the opposite characteristics) are: backward, boorish, dull, inept, ignorant, uncultivated, simple, garish, or tacky.

Because this is your life, you get to choose, and I vote for love your SMART self.

Your breath knows you are smart and it shows up 24/7 just to keep you alive...so....

1. Start with one breath at a time. Think about your breathing, and consciously count three slow, deep breaths. Bring the breath into your belly first, as if you are filling a glass of water, and then exhale starting at the top of your lungs until they are empty. Then fill your belly again and repeat three times. Do this exercise whenever you think about it throughout the day.

2. Choose your thoughts carefully and with intention. Remind yourself that: "Right Thought" creates "Right Speech" and "Right Speech" sets the stage for "Right Action." Use these tools when stepping out into the world.

3. Check your thinking, and make it positive whenever you notice it is getting negative.

4. Remind yourself that you are indeed smart and learning to love all aspects of yourself.

5. Stay vigilant of your thinking whether by yourself, in your work, or with your family and loved ones. By keeping your thoughts, your speech, and your actions positive and compassionate, you will continually open the door to tomorrow with grace and gratitude.

6. Give yourself the positive messages to encourage and continue the change for your well-being and your success.

7. Each time you acknowledge a loving part of yourself, you are building strong skills to Love YOU.

When you need a gentle reminder, use SMART to mean:

S...Some

M...Mental

A...Alerts

R...Require

T...Tenderness

Chapter 6

Exercise Willingness Rather Than Will Power

If you can't imagine yourself in a state of well-being, in control of and engaged in your life, what we are calling your sober self, your healthy self, then take those adjectives and make them verbs. How about sobering yourself, or healing yourself, and then loving the results? Can you begin to imagine yourself getting healthy and sober? Can you picture yourself acting in life without the familiar behaviors that perpetuate your unhealthy habits and addictions? Can you think about what you felt like when you were radiantly healthy and sober in the past? Are you beginning to have a vision of yourself as healthy, active, and flourishing in life? Will you give up thinking of yourself as: loser, idiot, stupid, a hopeless addict, or any other descriptive idea you can collect from the past?

If "Yes," is your answer, then you are on your way to creating something wonderful in your life. It must be an unequivocal "Yes." No cheating on this one, because what you think about is exactly what you will achieve. When you realize the significance and the power of your thinking and your thoughts, I promise you, many aspects of your life will change.

If "No" is your answer; if you are not ready to stop thinking about your addiction as "running your life" and your sobriety is never going to be a lifestyle; if you are not willing to give up the "critical self," the "judging self," and the "hard on yourself" self, then we have to do some more creative problem-solving. Take Mary's addiction to food, for example.

> *No matter how much she ate, she never felt full or satisfied. Her addiction to sugar and white flour had taken over her life. She would think about the cookies and cakes stashed in her desk during work, and then imagine the shopping spree on her way home. Her weight had begun to creep up on the scale and she toyed with the idea of purging the sweets before taking on the next course. For some reason, she was never able to get herself to throw up, and so she continued to beat herself up for such a lack of willpower. At this point in her life, she was not even willing to consider the ideas from* Love YOU, *in fact, she hated herself.*

Maybe it isn't a matter of hard work and willpower; maybe it is just as easy as knowing you want and deserve to be loved by you, and that simply takes acceptance. Accepting what is going on is the first step in claiming your willingness to do something differently in order to find what you are capable of.

It is not impossible for you to achieve that desired sober, healthy self; you just have to want it and *believe you deserve to have what you want.* Some of us have to be willing to be willing, and you can add as many willings as you would like. Then, give yourself the time to accept that someday, you will arrive at yes.

Now let's take the yes and move to the love piece. Here you can certainly come to an understanding of compassion and empathy. Think of your best friends, loved ones, children, relatives, or even a favorite pet; in short, those you love and those who love you back. Go ahead—actually bring them into your imagination. You can even recall that special someone who thought you were just terrific (the person we discussed in Chapter Four). That person validated you in the past, and now you can acknowledge how important they were in your life by remembering the care they offered you.

Can you remember the feeling of loving those people, of caring for them, of saying words and doing things you loved doing for them? Can you conjure up the feeling of how much you cared, no matter what happened, and how you were there for them and would always go that extra mile?

Take that feeling, the one of love, caring, compassion, empathy, and kindness, and hold on to your seatbelt. I am going to ask you to do something with that feeling you just recreated. Can you sense that feeling of love and compassion in your body? Can you feel it in your heart? Can you make it stronger when you think of how much you truly love those people (or even pets)?

Now, take that feeling and pour it all over yourself. That's right. Simply take the feeling as if it were a glorious waterfall and allow it to bathe you in the feeling of love. Simply sit in the energy of the love you just created!

Now there you have it—Love YOU...You're off to a great start!

The Alcoholics Anonymous 12-step program encourages a belief in a higher power. The program asks members to believe in something greater than themselves. A Force, a Source of Energy, Nature, the Universe, God, Spirit, a Higher Power that will support and assist them in finding a healthy, peaceful, and sober way of living in the world.

For some, the idea of a higher power was never part of their upbringing and others might have abandoned the idea for very good reasons.

What if you were willing to simply replace all the negative ideas of what a higher power is with a belief in a greater source of energy for yourself? How about simply, love? Trust that there is a love for you from a very basic place in your inner being, and it has always been there. You have, without a doubt, that great source of energy available to you. You will be able to cultivate the belief in yourself by loving yourself first. Love YOU is where you begin.

Here's a dialogue that Jack shared. For him, the realization came through a most unusual connection of truths.

Jack, a father of two beautiful daughters, was in treatment for drug and sex addiction. He hated himself. He absolutely despised where his addiction had taken him. He had broken every moral value he had ever been taught. At one point, he confided in his group, "I feel like I have raw sewage running through my veins. I have no soul. I feel completely unlovable after what I have done." Jack's counselor started to ask him questions:

Counselor: "Do you love your little girls who are four and six?"

Jack: "Of course."

Counselor: "How much, Jack?"

Jack: "More than I have ever loved anything."

Counselor: "If one of your little girls confided in you that she had committed a terrible crime, would you still love her?"

Jack: "Yes, I suppose I would."

Counselor: "OK, now think about your version of a Higher Power. Does your Higher Power love you the way a parent loves a child?"

Jack: "Yes, I suppose it does."

Counselor: "Let me get this straight; others love you unconditionally, your Higher Power loves you unconditionally, but you can't love yourself. Now that's an amazing ego you have. What makes you so much

more unlovable than anyone else? Truth is you
aren't. You just think you are...."

And just like that, Jack suddenly saw the lie his
brain had been telling him. It was time to start loving
himself. After all, if other people, even his Higher
Power could love him, why couldn't he love himself?

In Loving YOU, you must acknowledge that in the past you have tried too hard, much too hard! There is an uncomplicated way to successful sobriety and a healthy, fulfilling life

To Love YOU is to learn how to allow yourself, at a subconscious level, to create a new image; one that is absolutely necessary for positive change. Then, comfortable sobriety and health will happen naturally.

♦ Loving YOU makes it possible for you to operate a previously hidden series of controls and to activate some that have not existed before, at least not until now.

♦ Loving YOU sends a powerful message to your computer-like brain. Once you learn to operate it, and then trust it, there'll be no stopping you.

♦ Loving YOU is a wonderful shift of feelings. In comparison to reading music note by note and counting every beat, to Love YOU is like flying on the wings of a song.

♦   Loving YOU is like driving on cruise control. You are still in charge of the machine, but loving yourself makes it easy and comfortable.

All that trying in your past has not been wasted. Nothing ever goes to waste. Have you ever noticed you can absorb all kinds of facts, and then suddenly when you learn one more fact, everything comes together? Loving YOU can do that for you with all you've learned through past experiences, and make it automatic, thus easy, comfortable, and joyous.

Loving YOU is automatic; an educated instinct, and a built-in confidence. It's the kind of instinct you may have lost; the instinct experts say children use when choosing what they want to eat when they are given a variety of healthy foods. You'll like learning to trust your body and your instincts.

Comfortable goes with easy. Let's talk about comfort, the last thing you expect while on a journey toward healthy habits and sobriety. Paradoxically, the more comfort you can create for yourself, the smoother any program will move along. Comfortable is like wearing old bedroom slippers and feeling good about having them in your closet. They are a pleasure to slip into at the end of a long day. Your toes sing with the space and softness they offer. Easy gives the idea of lack of difficulty or anxiety, that something can be achieved without a lot of effort or struggle. When you put "easy" and "comfortable" together, the human heart is happy because there is lightness and a possibility of being successful; easy and comfortable means you will stick to the plan.

Whenever you try too hard to do something, you become tense and rigid, but everything comes more easily when you relax. You are the only one who can identify your comfort index.

If Loving YOU or the idea of loving yourself is a new idea, then approach the concept with ease and curiosity. Once you learn you can trust yourself, you may choose to manage your behavior and plan who you will hang out with, where you will go, when you will practice self-care, and how you will treat yourself and others.

Your desire for health will arrive at the Love YOU level, a place where both your intention for well-being and healthy behaviors will merge into success. At that same spot, you will be urged to consider yourself worth pampering, you will learn how to discover what actually pleasures you, and you will discover what you can achieve by giving yourself what you really want.

This is not a self-love that becomes narcissistic and selfish; all that is too obsessive and just too much work. Work is the last thing you want to do. "Try" is a word from the past! "Try" is an old tape. Here, you are simply going to "give it a go!"

Love Your Steadfast Self

Sixteen Ways to Stay the Course, Prevent Relapse

What about relapse? We work three steps forward and sometimes six steps back. Relapse is a constant companion and a dreaded secret lie. Keep her out in the open by talking about all the components and the seductive strategies relapse employs. David's story is much too familiar and heartbreaking.

> *Cocaine demands more than everything. At some point or another, the love affair with such a powerful drug takes your soul and your spirit. David started using pot when he was in high school and picked up cocaine in his twenties. He had been able to manage a very successful career, but lost custody of his three children in a very bitter divorce. Now forty, he is in recovery, working the AA program, touching base with his sponsor daily, attending meetings and "slipping" on a regular basis. He has not been sober for more than sixty days in the past five years. What else could the drugs take from him? There is not much left.*

The most challenging component of Loving YOU is the impulse of engaging in your unhealthy habits, behaviors, and addiction. Relapsing happens when you least expect it. If you have a plan and anticipate what might, could, or would happen when you are not looking, then you will make the right choice.

If you have read Judith Viorst children's book *Alexander and the Terrible, Horrible, No-Good, Very Bad Day*, you'll remember how the author reminds us, "Some days are like that. Even in Australia." But that's all they are: days that don't go the way you want them to go. At the end of the day, you get to go to sleep and wake up to start another day, with a new attitude, rejuvenated enthusiasm, and a cultivated aliveness that encourages good decision-making. When you are loving yourself you will hear the deep, quiet voice inside of you that whispers: "You are healthy, well, and sober!"

That feeling of believing in yourself is always available to you when you love yourself. That is the basis for the foundation of staying the course. It doesn't matter that you are struggling one more day, one more hour, or even one more minute. What does matter is that you get to have access to that feeling of pride and accomplishment. You are sober.

How do you know you love yourself? The only way you choose to stay sober, and it is a choice, is one day at a time. That one day of sobriety is an act of self-love. That one day becomes one week, two months, ten years. You build all the days of sobriety behind you, and you know in your very cells of your being that your sense of accomplishment has been because you are steadfast and loving yourself. Here are fifteen relapse prevention strategies, tools you can also use to keep your focus on a healthy path:

1. Relapse is real and always lingering at the doorstep of your mind. Make a decision to stay healthy and sober.

2. Have a plan that will address any situation that might cause you to backslide. Use critical thinking so you avoid your unhealthy habits, behaviors, and addictions.

3. Be prepared to ask yourself these kinds of questions:

    ◆   What to do when life doesn't go my way?

    ◆   What to do when I feel disappointment in others?

    ◆   What to think, do, or say when I am so angry?

    ◆   What to do when I am so stressed and exhausted?

    ◆   How to take care of myself when I am taking care of everyone else?

    ◆   What to say when someone offers me a drink and I am sober?

    ◆   Where to find a quiet place to just think for a minute?

    ◆   What to do when my brother comes to the house stoned?

    ◆   What could I do when I am feeling vulnerable, tired, lonely, sad, or hungry?

4. Then rehearse, rehearse, rehearse. Replay your answers to those questions and you will be prepared.

5. Decide if you are motivated by the proverbial carrot or the stick. Make a list of all the things from which you will benefit when you are leading a healthy and sober life. Make a list of all the things you will lose if you do not stay sober. Read the list daily!

6. Become a student of your own impulses and design a plan to implement for individual impulse control. Impulse starts in your body and before you know it, you will have made the phone call, eaten the candy, bought the booze, placed the bet, or slept with someone...without thinking. Know your triggers! Study them, tell your friends to watch out for the signs, and know that impulse is lurking around every corner. Just put the brakes on and give yourself time.

7. Learn to make space in your thinking, in your feelings, in your actions, in your speaking, in your life...in other words, slow down and breathe.

8. When your body is having sensations like shakiness, nervousness, anxiety, panic, nausea, worry, then stop...stop...and place your hand over your heart. Feel your own warmth and the beating of your heart. Sense the self-love you can conjure up and send it towards yourself. You will be giving

yourself an opportunity to respond rather than react.

9.   Remind yourself on a regular basis that your health and sobriety are your priorities.

10. Remind yourself that you are accessing the pride you have for your own personal accomplishment of staying healthy and sober. You are loving yourself for one more day of health and sobriety; truly an act of love.

11. Figure out exactly what it would take to backslide and relapse. One more drink, one more pill, one more scratch ticket, one more date, one extra hour of work, one more quart of ice cream, just a few minutes on the Internet, just one small Hershey's Kiss®, and then remind yourself that all your effort, sincere wanting, and sense of accomplishment and pride will all go away and you will have to start all over again.

12. Being sober and healthy is a one-time gift, similar to the air you breathe. The gift of life arrived when you took your first breath and, as a cherished gift, it keeps on giving. For many of us, sobriety and well-being is not handed to us on a silver platter. You worked hard to live healthy and sober, and you don't want to simply throw it away for a moment of addictive pleasure. Learn to hold your sobriety and well-being as a precious gift. When you

cherish your well-being, nothing can take it from you.

13. Remember the pain—all of it—addiction and self-destructive habits have a very clever way of making you forget the pain and minimize the suffering. In fact, addiction comes with a built-in forgetter. Have the courage to remember the pain.

14. Find a community to support your sobriety and your wellness; whether it's family, friends, AA, OA, SLAA, ACOA, NA, or GA. The *Big Book* from Alcoholics Anonymous says we can't summon up with enough force the memory of the pain; we need to hear the stories all over again. We are also not alone in this journey, so reach out for the support, friendship, and encouragement you deserve to have.

15. Be honest with how bad your life has been and love the part of you that is truly sincere. Put your hand over your heart when you are saying to yourself or others, "Oh, it wasn't so bad." But understand it really was and is bad; that is one of the reasons you are reading this book. Feel the disconnect in your body and know that you are choosing to stay healthy and sober one more day.

16. Recovery and wellness happens in your body and in your gut. Stay present in your body through awareness, mindfulness practice, and breathing. Listen to your body, hear that quiet voice that

says, "You are healthy, well, and sober and I am here for you." Stay that way!

Christopher's diligent commitment to his own sobriety put loving himself in a very clear perspective. His wisdom and willingness to share reinforces the paramount value of loving yourself first.

One of the many paradoxes in 12-step recovery surrounds the notion of selfishness. On the one hand, we are told and must admit that what fuels our addiction is, at base, selfishness. Alcoholic Anonymous uses the Big Book *and for example, tells us, "selfishness or self-centeredness" is at the core of our addictions! And then we think that selfishness is the root of our troubles. Driven by a hundred forms of fear, self-delusions, self-seeking, and self-pity, we step on the people we love and they retaliate. So, admitting and redressing this major character defect is essential to any long-term sobriety. But then we come into the program and one of the first things we hear is, "It's a selfish program. Put yourself first!" This paradox can be confusing and off-putting to the newcomer.*

Upon reflection, however, we discover that this really is no paradox at all, or rather, just a semantic one. The trick to resolving it is understanding that the word "selfish" as used in the two contexts; the one that drives our disease, and the one that drives our program of recovery refer to two entirely different ideas. The selfishness as the root of our troubles is egocentric and is, in fact, a character defect. We protect our addiction at all costs, including lying and completely disregarding the wishes and feelings of others. It is well-defined in the Big Book *as "self-delusion, self-seeking, and self-pity." It's ugly stuff.*

The so-called selfishness used in the phrase, "It's a selfish program," however, gestures towards a completely different concept. Like the "selfishness" involved in a parent's putting on the airplane's oxygen mask before putting on the child's, "selfishness" in 12-step recovery is a life-saving and self-loving act. If we don't put our recovery first and take care of our sobriety on a daily basis, we will perish. So next time you hear, "It's a selfish program," think instead that it's a self-preserving program, because that is what's really meant. Being selfish in recovery—that is putting on our own oxygen mask first, is an essential act of Loving YOU!

Chapter 7

Just Maybe Your Mother Was Wrong

During the formative years, or the early years of childhood, we are most vulnerable to what happens in our relationships with our caretakers. The messages and interactions from the elders we love and trust will have an impact on us during our preteen years and the tender time in young adulthood.

Whether in the home, at school, in a place of worship, at the playground, or on the streets; when we are young, we assess how the world works. We operate our perceptions of reality from the frame of reference we adopted growing up.

As children, our biggest fear is being left with no one to take care of us. It is almost impossible to find a family that is constantly encouraging, supportive, trustworthy, kind, unconditionally loving, and focused on the goals of helping each individual be the best they can be and without judgment. So, since most of us have come from families that fall short of perfect, we have a collective challenge ahead; a challenge to go forth without criticism, or judgment; without words that twist and turn your perception of who you are in the world. In short, a challenge to practice loving ourselves unconditionally!

Consider thinking of the beginning of your life as a baby. You came into this world as royalty, either a king or a queen, and you knew that you were precious and special. Possibly up to the age of three, as you explored your environment and ventured out into the world, you lived a life out of love and joy. Nothing could stop your enthusiasm to learn to talk, walk, and figure out what made you happy. You spent all your time managing your body in relationship to all that was around you. You were consumed with eating, pooping, crying, laughing, sleeping, and trusting that you would be safe and loved.

We took in the messages that many of us received with an open heart. Those messages could have been directly said, inadvertently implied, or even delivered by circumstance, ancillary relationships or unexplained events of the past. At such tender ages, all that was said and implied to us settled in our bones and then into the nooks and crannies of our very souls. Those messages moved our being and our behaviors in possible directions, either negatively towards struggle and future heartache, or positively, allowing our inner light to shine, supporting our success and ease in life.

If you were given the message that you were not good enough, not strong enough, not fast enough, not smart enough, not talented enough, then your inner self constantly struggles to "fix" itself to meet those expectations.

When you were told that you couldn't do it right, when you wrote with the wrong crayon or didn't stay in the lines; when you couldn't read fast enough or didn't get the perfect grade, or were told you were stupid; you took those words and cemented a yellow brick road that you are still walking, hoping it will get you to where you want to be.

Coming face-to-face with the understanding that those statements and those directions; those criticisms were not given in your best interest, but given out of frustration, anger, and shame by the caretakers in your life who were responsible for your well-being.

Often you don't begin to realize until adulthood that the statements you heard as a child were raw, painful, damaging, and just *wrong.*

Thus we have the birth of those internal gremlins: The critical voices, recordings, tapes, and messages that seem to run continually as background noise in our lives. Sometimes your internal dialogue is so subtle that you don't recognize the impact until it is just too late. You take on the negative and critical belief and operate from a place unloving towards yourself. We are not looking to play a blame game here; the past is over and now we can move forward with enthusiasm to begin to solve the problem and bring a new way of being to your life.

It doesn't make the person who might have perpetrated the violent language or behavior a bad person; they did the best they could given the limitations they had at that time in their life. We spend most of our lives working to resolve and heal the relationships we had with our caretakers. Any awareness you can claim will assist you in your process to integrate the past into a healthy and sober life ahead. Knowing that our journey demands healing of the past, we can find the courage to move forward and change the messages of our history.

Your body holds all your past memories and can give you the clues to open yourself to healing. The memories are hidden behind the ache in your heart or the burning in your stomach, the tightness in your throat, and the tears in your eyes. You will find memories in a tight shoulder or under the pressure in your back, bruises on your arms and the feeling of tingling in your head. When you sit with the sensations, breathe slowly and consciously, then ask yourself when the first time was that you noticed that feeling in your body; you just might come up with a memory from your childhood. That memory will give you a clue as to how you can begin to rewrite the script of your past.

We might find that we spend our lives trying to be the best, and are often critical that nothing is good enough. We might be consumed with trying to reach the highest peak in our professional or personal lives, reflective that we were never given acknowledgment and recognition for the efforts we displayed as youngsters. It is painful when we come face-to-face with the truth that the caretakers who criticized us, and demeaned us, and limited us, were simply wrong.

Your memories will assist you in understanding why you have been making unhealthy choices in your life. Even during your attempts to maintain sobriety, people in your life whom you trusted and loved have sometimes fallen short in their unconditional support and love. The statements that make you feel like a loser, or unloved, or that you will never be successful, or that you are defective, are simply wrong, even when you hear them as an adult. Once you believe that you are more than what other people think of you, and that the love for yourself is growing, history will turn on its heels and you will have the opportunity to redo and reinvent the past.

You have the power to drop the statements of criticism, negativity, and discouragement, and replace them with the positive messages and affirmations that make it possible for healing renewal and new directions.

Love Your Scared Self

How to Reinforce Your Inner Courage

Listen to your inner dialogue—the words you say to yourself—and ask if the words are familiar and possibly from your youth. "I'm too scared." "It's too much." "I am frightened." "It's overwhelming." "Please, don't ask me to do that." "I'm afraid I won't do it right." "Something bad will happen...I'm really scared." "I'm frozen in fear." And so on.

The fear we all carry around can stop us in our tracks and certainly prevent us from moving forward. The part of you that is scared, anxious, frightened, jittery, uneasy, nervous, agitated, worried, apprehensive, fearful, terrified, uncertain, threatened, and overwhelmed, needs only for you to acknowledge the feeling and then make friends with it. Yes, exactly; make friends with your fear almost as if you are building a new relationship.

Turn this stranger into a friend just like you would do with a new acquaintance. Think of the last person you met that has now become a friend. I am sure there was some apprehension with the first meeting. Perhaps it was a co-worker, or a boss, or a child from the neighborhood, maybe a client or a customer or the person who has become your life partner.

You spent some time together and got to know each other. Through dialogue and storytelling, you measure up whether or not you would like to pursue the relationship. You can do the same thing with your fear if you are willing to think differently about getting to know that side of yourself.

Fear is an important feeling of energy that gives you some feedback as to using caution and having realistic expectations about a situation. Smart women and men know their limitations and won't put themselves in harm's way if they can help it. But the everyday fears that stop us from doing what we really want to do and living a life of enrichment and fulfillment can be harnessed and put to better use by loving that feeling and making friends with the fear.

Love your scared self with unconditional ease and compassion. You might say something like: "Oh, here comes my fear, you poor dear, and I will love you unconditionally so you can assist me in the next step towards my growth and my happiness."

To help reinforce your inner courage and truth, try these statements on for size:

- I am capable.
- I can do this.
- I have it in me.
- I have a talent.
- I am enough just the way I am.
- I am strong.
- I am smart.
- I am determined.
- I am vibrant and creative.
- I have energy.
- I have what it takes to make wise choices for a full and healthy life.

Chapter 8

Would You Sabotage Yourself to Make Her Right?

It is certainly possible that you have ventured into health and sobriety and after a short while found yourself back in the middle of self-destructive habits and a harmful addictive cycle. Because even though the past is over, you are still good at bringing up the memories of self-abuse, self-criticism, and wrenching shame. How many times have you called yourself "stupid" for making the decision to sacrifice your well-being, your health, and your sobriety and then spiraled down into yet another dark hole?

The pain might be right on the surface and the suffering could go deep. Regardless, the discomfort and hurt can initiate feelings of shame, guilt, embarrassment, and desperation; all the ingredients of what it takes to beat yourself up and feel lousy. Thoughts of what others have said about you begin to take form and you hear in your head: "I guess she was right." "They told me I couldn't't do it." "No wonder she didn't believe me when I told her that this time I was serious." "No one will even want to talk to me again." "I'll never be able to show my face." "No one will ever trust me."

"Nobody loves me, everybody hates me, I might as well go out and eat worms!"

Charlene's return to her addiction to alcohol brought her ongoing heartache and struggle. It wasn't until she began to even consider the tremendous loss of her relationship with her own children that she was willing to act towards loving herself from a healthy and sober place.

Here is the beginning of her story:

Charlene grew up the middle girl with four brothers and two sisters. Drinking since adolescence, she stopped for a period of ten years to have children and raise a family. Her husband was now in recovery and no longer drinking, so it made no sense why she began using alcohol again. Life had become more than unmanageable, and at the age of thirty-eight, she was drinking daily. The hangovers often made getting to work a challenge, but more than that, her interactions with the children caused heartache and stress for the entire family.

Her patience was short and her temper hot—and everyone knew it. Her daughter had just entered the community college and her two high school-age sons spent most of their time at school with sports and music. Both Charlene's personal and professional lives were desperately feeling the consequences of her addiction.

Arguments with her husband were bitter and loud, with little resolution. Her bottle of wine in the even-

ing turned to two and sometimes three, and she was
often asleep on the couch before the kids got home.
No one wanted to rock her boat and instead they left
her in isolation and often would exclude her from
events. Her behavior had become embarrassing to
everyone.

Similar to Charlene, you might begin to ask yourself the questions that cause even more heartache: "Why did I do it again?" "Why can't I just stop spending money, eating sugar, using those pain pills, drinking wine every night, over eating, gambling, working too much, fighting, using the internet, buying clothes and shoes, and so on?" "What's wrong with me anyway?" "How can I continue to be so stupid?"

This is a good time for you to take a slow, deep, full breath. That's right—just breathe. You might as well get used to doing it while you are reading this book, because you will incorporate the skill of breathing into the fabric of your healthy and sober life.

Now that you have had a moment to give space to the past and reflect on what is happening right now in your body, in your heart, and in your mind, ask yourself if there is a hint of evidence that you might be sabotaging yourself to make someone else right. Think about "sabotage" as a deliberate action of subversion or obstruction to weaken and disrupt your desire to live a healthy and fulfilling life. When your actions are not in your best interest and you are not making healthy choices, there is a chance that you are unconsciously sabotaging your own success.

If you have found yourself at the bottom of an unhealthy cycle of behavior over and over, someone or something is sabotaging your health and sobriety. It would be best to accept responsibility instead of blaming someone or something else. Your mother didn't make you drink and your boss doesn't make you use drugs. Your husband doesn't run up your credit card and your wife doesn't buy the ice cream. Your kids aren't the reason you are always working and your drug dealer doesn't just make house calls unannounced. You are responsible for your decisions, and some of them are mistakes—big mistakes, but that is all they are—mistakes.

Negative Self-Talk

One sure sign that the idea of Loving Yourself is not present in your life is all the negative self-talk going on inside your head. When it is loud and extreme, your willingness to be aware of what is going on takes mindful attention. At first I was shocked when I actually heard myself calling myself names right out loud. And not just in cases where such names might be warranted, but actually for silly stuff that happens to everyone, like forgetting something after I've left the house, dropping my keys, bumping into an open cabinet door, or spilling my tea.

Since thoughts create our reality, it's important to break this nasty habit. I heard someone share at a meeting that one day it occurred to him that he wouldn't tolerate anyone else calling him names the way he does to himself, so why should he tolerate them coming from his own mouth, brain, or mind? Why would I want to treat my friend so poorly? And if I am becoming my own best friend, it is time to pay attention to my inner dialogue. It's those gremlins at work. They love being able to upset your apple cart of living easily and effortlessly. The voices in your head are real enough to cause significant damage. With awareness and mindfulness, you can do something about it...after all, it's your head!

I try my best to catch myself engaging in negative self-talk, have a little chuckle, and turn it around with an affirmation. Here is a way to frame the feeling "stupid." Making mistakes can take on a new profile when you reframe the word STUPID. Consider deleting the word "stupid" from your consciousness, your vocabulary, and your life. Replace it with an acronym that might give you permission to love yourself unconditionally, where STUPID stands for:

S...Some
T...Trip
U...Ups
P...Postpone
I...Intelligent
D...Decisions

Some Trip Ups Postpone Intelligent Decisions

Write it on a card and post it all around your world. Memorize it, so the next time you use the word "stupid" it is not a direct insult to yourself. You can feel better about making mistakes. Isn't that a relief? Don't stop at shame, guilt, or embarrassment; just keep moving and doing. Pick yourself up, have a little chuckle, pat yourself on the back, and say, "Oops, that was a trip up."

The truth is that you talk to yourself in ways that you would never tolerate or allow someone else to speak to you. It's as if you are holding two telephone receivers to your ears and listening to an opposite message in each ear. The chatter can become destructive and you will begin to feel defeated. Be easy on yourself. Listen to what you are actually saying to yourself and if you are ready for change, your new encouraging words will usher that negative self-talk away.

Listen closely, so you can simply Love YOU.

Love Your Sabotaging Self

Ten Ways to Back Up the Hard Drive of Your Mind

When Charlene's children finally confronted her with their fears of losing her as a mother and a friend, she reached out for help and a friend took her to AA (Alcoholics Anonymous). She began attending AA meetings and entertained the idea of being healthy and sober. Her willingness

to be sober brought about the necessary actions that se-
cured a sponsor, a therapist, a good diet, a meditation practice, and a new beginning with her family. She never wants
to forget the past, so she can ensure a sober and healthy
future. Here is her hope for tomorrow:

> *"Sometimes I think it would be nice to have a glass*
> *of wine. It stinks that I can't even have one alcoholic*
> *drink. Then I remember it sucks more to be hung*
> *over with a throbbing headache, dehydrated, and so*
> *nauseated I can't eat or get out of bed. At that mo-*
> *ment, I realize 'I Love Me more than the drunk I once*
> *was.'"*

When your life is running smoothly and living with ease
becomes an everyday occurrence, practice gratitude. Success is the time to remind yourself that you deserve to Love
Yourself, not only for all the effort it has taken you to be
healthy and sober, but simply because you are who you
are.

There is a part of you that sits silent, watching and listening for an opportunity to show up with the intention to
divert you from making healthy choices. A "saboteur" willfully destroys. When you fall off the wagon, your sabotaging
self definitely destroys the sober streak you had going.
When you are "asleep" in life, or simply not paying attention
to the choices in your behavior, or when you are feeling
vulnerable to your inner critic, that's when the sabotaging
self enters the scene. It's an insidious part of you that is

susceptible and vulnerable to making unhealthy choices when things are going really well. It's the part that minimizes potential consequences and encourages you to act impulsively even when you know better. It's the part of yourself that patiently waits for you to doze off and forget where you've been and where you are headed.

We have talked about awareness and vigilance and how vital these skills are for your continued success. Knowing that there is a part of you that might feel less deserving, fearful, and intimidated by your well-being is half the battle. That sabotaging self is like a virus in your computer-like mind and will wipe out all your files with just a click of the mouse.

How many times have you lost an important document or (gasp!) all—and I mean *all*— of your information because you neglected to save and back up? Having had that experience, and let's face it, everyone has, do you now regularly save and back up the files on your computer? Without these precautionary measures, you are vulnerable to computer crashes, power surges, and old-fashioned accidents; and you risk ending up in a puddle of desperate remorse with no possibility to retrieve the lost information.

Create a method to secure your data and make backing-up a habit in order to keep your files safe. Recently, The Cloud has been the buzz of computer technology, as it allows you to access your data, files, and information remotely, from wherever you might be. In a metaphorical way, the same holds true in the world of this process of Loving YOU.

Self-love, confident personal self-worth, and positive self-esteem are becoming the internal files on the hard drive of your psyche. You have been putting in the effort to recognize that you are special and precious and that you are worth respect and love. And as a result of that effort, you can now access that positive thinking; that folder filled with love, wherever and whenever you need to.

Here are ten ways to create a simple and inexpensive back-up system for loving yourself:

1. Create a "Self-Love Box" and fill it with memories that will keep you loving yourself.

2. Write down things you have done in your life that made you feel proud. Jot notes about what people have said to you that made you feel great; keep thank-you cards, birthday cards, and love notes you receive from people you care about. Use the Self-Love Box to recharge love for yourself, reignite your inner glow, and on a challenging day, reboot your crashed system. The restorative function of a Self-Love Box is powerful!

3. Keep positive pictures of yourself available for viewing. Frame your favorites and place them in prominent positions in your home. Edit your Facebook and keep only healthy and sober pictures on your pages.

4. Write affirmations on small pieces of paper and tape them all around your world. Read them every day.

5. Frame your accomplishments. If you have a professional license or a degree, frame it and hang it in your room to remind you of your accomplishments and that you are someone important and completely lovable.

6. Develop a ritual every morning that will set your mind and your day on the right track. It could be a statement, a prayer, a meeting, a routine, a practice, a ceremony, a workout, or a hug, to reinforce your desire for an easy and joyous day ahead. When you open your eyes in the morning, make the first thought a positive and grateful one. Review your plans for the day with ease and gratitude, knowing that you "get to do it again," whatever "it" might be for you.

7. When you close your eyes before sleep, take stock of your progress and the healthy choices you made throughout the day. Remind yourself that by loving who you are, you reinforce the little decisions that keep you healthy, sober, and loving yourself.

8. Find a picture of someone who loves you dearly or has been an inspiration or a mentor in your life, maybe a grandparent, a teacher, a spiritual teacher, a famous author, or a charismatic leader. Post the picture in a prominent place and every time you glance at it, know that your "hard drive" of loving yourself is being backed up.

9. Pay attention to your breath. When you breathe in, you are taking a part of the loving, life energy source that is available to everyone, and when you breathe out, you are creating more space for yet more love. Simply let the idea ruminate in your heart area and you will feel the "back up drive" humming along.

10. Tell yourself that you are in love with you, and you are learning how to become your own best friend. Remind yourself that you have turned on the "back up" system and it is **Fail-Safe**.

Self-Love Is a Feeling and a Set of Actions

Matthew found health and sobriety through friends who were members of the AA program. He had been a drug user since his teens. Now at forty-eight years old, he was struggling to stay sober and to be present for his children and the family members that dearly loved him. Loving himself was never an option before and his behavior for more than twenty years had been risky, detrimental, and destructive to his life. The AA program, sponsors, and vigilant attention to his sobriety gave him a new chance to make healthy decisions for his recovery. His reflection about that struggle to come to love himself shows in his willingness to share his deep found wisdom:

"How do you know when you love yourself? Surely, there's an emotional component. I think we all know

when we feel love. But in the same way addicts must question their thoughts, we must also question our feelings. We are great self-deceivers, capable of delusions of both the thought and the feeling varieties.

"Is there another barometer of self-love beyond the ideas and feelings in our heads? Why, yes, there is: our actions in the world! Self-love involves a series of activities, including self-care, self-sensitivity, and self-respect. Do we think or speak badly about ourselves? Do we take care of personal hygiene and appearance? Do we take care of our health through our diet and exercise regimens? Do we treat ourselves with the same compassion and softness that we treat other loved ones in our lives? Looking honestly at our daily actions and measuring them against questions like these can reveal how far we've gone on the path and practicing the ideas in this little Love YOU book."

Chapter 9

Like a GPS in Your Head, Chatter Never Stops

If you are breathing, then your mind is making thoughts. It is what minds do. Your mind makes thoughts the way your heart pumps blood. You cannot tell your heart where to send the next pint of hemoglobin, but you can learn to quiet your mind and influence the direction of your thinking. That is very good news and it is the basis for hope, for change, and will support your efforts in learning how to Love YOU.

Take some time to think about how you are thinking and what the committee in your head is saying. Are the voices, those annoying gremlins, judging you, your actions, your behaviors, your wishes, hopes, and dreams? Is there planning going on and list-making happening? Might you be rehearsing and designing an upcoming conversation or reviewing one from the past? Are you daydreaming about the future or hoping and wishing that something might happen soon? Do you sometimes miss the exit while driving or walk into a room and forget why you are there? Have you ever had a thought so bizarre that you wanted to spend some time tracing it back to its origin? You might have been looking for your keys, and within a matter of seconds, you are thinking about the time your grandmother gave you a music box with a lock on it.

The mind is truly the greatest frontier, and learning to harness the power of your thinking can change your life for the better.

We are still trying to figure out how the mechanics of how our minds work. We know that somewhere, deep inside, there is a self that is yearning to be in charge. When we are young children we spend most of our time playing, and that play is designed to help us separate ourselves from others. The intention of our nature is to become independent, brave, and willing to develop the skills that will help us become who we were meant to be.

If we are unconditionally loved and nurtured, encouraged and supported, then over time we develop the skills that help us learn to make healthy choices in life.

Most of us can relate to the lack of that kind of early childhood experience. If we grew up in an invalidating environment where we felt criticized, judged, and shamed, we could have developed an external vigilance of watching what is going on with others instead of with ourselves. We became vigilant because we were always trying to satisfy someone else's expectations and it didn't matter what we thought about ourselves.

A child is an artist until he is told he is not.
~John Lennon

If we are always scanning for danger, it is very challenging to relax into love.

Appoint yourself the chairman of the board, the leader of the pack, the president of the corporation, and the star of the show...*your* show. Make it your job to get all the thoughts, voices, and dialogues in your head on the same page. Make sure they are reading from the same script and are familiar with the same mission: your health, well-being, and sobriety.

When what you want becomes a priority, you are truly in charge and the one ordering lunch. You might not be able to control the thoughts, but how you handle the information, what you do with the chatter, and how you direct the action is absolutely your choice.

Remind all the parts of you that you are healthy, well, and learning to become your own best friend. Loving YOU is the framework for the GPS in your head, and that love will function successfully.

Now that you've set your GPS to health and well-being, let's reinforce the idea with that memory of someone from your early years who thought you were amazing. Someone in your past thought you were the best thing in the world. You felt noticed and acknowledged, supported and loved. It might have been a relative or a neighbor, a teacher at school, or the owner of the local bakery, perhaps a spiritual teacher, or what AA calls, "Your Higher Power as You Know It." An energy source that knows you are precious and worthy of a life of joy and ease.

Just like your car's GPS system, which is hooked into the satellite systems orbiting earth, the GPS in your head is hooked into an extensive database filled with unconditional love. You can trust the GPS to get you where you want to go because you trust the information to be precise and always available.

> *Laurie loved her grandmother growing up and has a fond memory of the times they would play cards together. There was an unspoken respect for each other and her commitment to being present in her Nana's life gave Laurie a sense of validation she had forgotten.*
>
> *"Nana would light up when I came into the room. She was my best cheerleader, and no matter what I was doing, she would always listen to me and tell me to be brave and go for what I truly wanted." Laurie never remembers having a trusting relationship with her mother or others in her life. She was not protected, and suffered many childhood traumas, which required tender attention later during her journey towards recovery from a life addicted to prescription medication. Sending an anchor back to the love her grandmother held for her gave Laurie permission to begin loving herself.*

Your internal GPS holds the memories of those who thought you were the best and who had faith in you right from the beginning. They remind you of your worthiness and Love YOU unconditionally. That awareness of your preciousness and individual magnificence has always been there, circling your life, like the satellites in space. It is time for you to hook into the energy and believe that you deserve a healthy, happy, and sober life.

As you continue to learn how to Love YOU, you will relax into the supportive energy of love, and the idea that your success is always possible with the very next breath.

Love Your Smiling Self

S.O.S. (Smile on Stress)

S.O.S., or Smile on Stress, is a strategy for everyone. Using your imagination, think of something that is pleasant and delightful, and see yourself smiling. The tiny muscles in your face will respond without your even knowing about them. Something happens in your brain that sends a signal to release the hormones that help you relax. Then, take a deep, easy breath and say to yourself, "My thoughts are clear and my body is relaxed." As you exhale, imagine warm energy flowing throughout your body. When you smile on the inside, the outside world changes. The same smile works when you encounter a stressful situation. The practice of smiling on the inside will set you up for a new way of dealing with the stress in your life. With enough practice, yes, daily practice, the stressful event will trigger an inner smile, and your inner smile will trigger freedom from stress. The conscious mind will remind you that you can do only one thing at a time: stress or smile. If you experiment with only this strategy, you will have a preview of the success you can expect from *Love YOU*. When you smile in response to stress, you are Loving YOU. Stress can be managed, reduced, and even transformed to work *for* you rather than against you.

How do you deal with the stress in your life? Do you know what the stress looks, feels, and even sounds like? Perhaps you would consider taking stock of your unconscious behaviors that play a deceptive part in making you think you are dealing with the stress?

What are the tensions and stressors, the adverse conditions, which cause you to anesthetize yourself through unhealthy behaviors and unsafe addictions? When you are so removed from your body and the present moment, eating, drugging, drinking, spending, gambling, and so on, might bring temporary relief, but your life becomes unmanageable and your unhealthy habits are not making things any better.

Take a look at Frank's life. Sitting on the sidelines, watching his children grow up without him, working himself to exhaustion and living in a fog of television haze.

TV consumed Frank's time and then his life. There was a television in every room and often he would watch two shows at once. Sporting events were the easiest to watch; especially when they were teams Frank was betting on.

The children would no longer pester him to play ball

or a board game. They knew he couldn't even pay attention to them when they wanted to talk, because the TV had to keep playing. Frank worked hard all day long and he felt he deserved to relax in the evening. Dinner and TV were exactly what he wanted and he was beginning to pay a high price.

He no longer knew what was happening with the children. His wife rarely talked to him. She had set up the spare room for herself with her own TV. They were living as roommates with little connection.

Chapter 10

Trade in Those Familiar Bedroom Slippers

When feeling sleepy, you are not alert and awake.

When feeling sluggish, you have no energy to move forward.

When feeling shy, you are reluctant to step forward into life.

When feeling strange, you are not comfortable with change.

When feeling scattered, you are not focused with intention.

And when you are loving all those parts of yourself, you can orchestrate a concerted effort towards acceptance and awareness of what it takes to Love YOU.

There is a cost when you allow your unhealthy habits to take you away from flourishing in life. Henry's unconscious choices for the familiar left him out of the game of life.

Henry's comfortable, familiar "bedroom slippers" are scratch tickets. He buys a lot of them. Occasionally he will save up to buy that lottery ticket he is hoping to score big with. His car is strewn with rejects and

his habit is fed with the winnings of a couple of
bucks here and there. He travels after work to vari-
ous towns in order to buy from a variety of conven-
ience stores in hopes that his luck will soon turn
around. Chasing the dream of winning and the thrill
of scratching a match seems to help him reduce the
stress in his life. He lives alone and has no interest
in spending time with friends or family. It's better
this way; he doesn't have to be social or friendly,
just lonely.

Routines are familiar, and old habits and rituals can become very comfortable. Your unhealthy habits are ol' buddies who have found a permanent home in your life and are eager to strike up a conversation at any time.

You and your habits and addictions have established routines together, and those routines and rituals have developed into habits that run easily on automatic pilot. For example, if wine is your best friend, you might routinely think about how that first glass will taste while you are driving home from work. If gambling is your addiction, you might have a routine of buying scratch tickets on a certain day or decide when to go to the casino. If food is your weakness, then your routine might include consuming sugar, pastries, and ice cream before bed every night, and no one knows but you that the chocolate is hiding in the freezer. Rituals include hiding places and destinations, phone calls and stomping grounds. Pot under the mattress, work meetings during your vacation, fifteen drafts of a letter before it is perfect, bills that never get paid, or too many un-explained backaches in order to secure another prescription.

Imagine a pair of favorite bedroom slippers that got so old and worn they actually molded to your feet. You can almost imagine how comfortable and familiar they would feel. Who would ever want to throw such comfort away? Those slippers are the most comfortable things you own. But are they practical, and will they take you to where you want to go? Old bedroom slippers are familiar, similar to the routines, rituals, and habits of automatic pilot; you don't have to think, they just fit so perfectly.

When you know you have chosen to go down a new path, the old slippers will never carry you across the terrain. You decide that you are ready for some new shoes, and often, new shoes will never feel as comfortable as those old slippers. They might hurt a bit and cramp your toes. New shoes might give you blisters and look weird on your feet. Well, it is the same with a healthy lifestyle. At first, having health and being sober might feel strange and pinch your soul. Making healthy choices might look a little weird and cause you to develop new habits, routines, and rituals that will certainly challenge your body, mind, and spirit.

You don't go out onto the ice and snow wearing sandals.

You don't wear hiking boots to swim with the dolphins.

You'd never wear high heels on a golf course.

You wouldn't wear flip-flops to the opera.

You wouldn't wear sneakers to go rock climbing.

But you might wear cowboy boots to bed!

When you Love YOU, you will trade in those old familiar bedroom slippers for shoes that will carry you into a healthy way of being. As you hike the terrain of sobriety, you will stay awake to the automatic pilot of routines, rituals, and habits. With new habits, routines, and rituals, you will learn to make healthy choices, have fewer problems, and leave your familiar bedroom slippers of unhealthy habits and addictions behind.

Our friend Jack, from above, learned a lot about how to love himself when he was in treatment, except he also made a few miscalculations. After a sixty-day stint in rehab, he decided to re-immerse himself into the same system he had just left. He went home to the same family, the same job, the same routine and all the same stimuli he had left. In a very short time, he was back doing the very same dangerous behaviors he was doing before, using cocaine and women as his crutch to survive. In the program of Alcoholics Anonymous there is a truth: "The only thing that needs to change is everything." This couldn't have been truer for Jack.

Jack decided to enter a long-term program to remove himself from his old environment and re-program his behaviors that had brought him to his bottom. There was only one problem: he hated *the program. He was doing things completely differently; communication with his family was cut off, he wasn't working seventy hours per week, he wasn't talking with his old friends, he had a completely new routine—for a long time—six months. In the beginning this was awful. The pain that Jack felt about being ripped out of his old system was immense, but as new, healthy behaviors took root, life became more comfortable one day at a time. Soon enough, Jack realized that he was going to be OK, despite not having his old crutches of co-dependency, sex, and drugs; his old comfortable bedroom slippers.*

One thing Jack learned in this process was that early on, comfortable stuff was dangerous. If he was feeling comfortable, he was caught in the old behavior. What was old got him in trouble. Instead, he was encouraged to do things differently; to do something new, and most importantly, to think long and hard about those things he knew he needed to do that scared him. Those were precisely the things he needed to pursue. Jack learned that this process is simple and often times not easy. It's messy, it hurts, it is cumbersome, but he needed to learn to love his Sleepy, Sluggish, Shy, Strange, Scattered Self...

Love Your Sleepy, Sluggish, Shy, Strange, Scattered Self

Four Simple Statements to Get You Up and Going

Can you relate to the times when you have absolutely no energy, no enthusiasm, no drive, no get-up-and-go-*oomph*? Has it been right after a difficult night or a stressful experience? Perhaps it was during a depressive episode or an exhausting emotional battle with yourself or others. No matter what is happening, you have a choice to change the behavior that is running the emotional roller coaster.

When you are having a hard time getting up in the morning or attempting to do something that feels impossible, there are four statements that will help. It doesn't matter what the challenge is, or how difficult the task might seem, just learn the statements by heart and say them often. Almost by magic, you will feel a surge of energy and encouragement from your inner self cheering you on.

The statements have only four words and the emphasis depends on how you say the phrase...over and over again. Practice saying them out loud and check your body. Notice how you are feeing with each word as you give more power and *oomph* to it!

I can do this.

I **CAN** do this.

I can **DO** this.

I can do **THIS**.

Chapter 11

Invite Yourself to Be Responsible for Your Life

Usually an invitation is a request urging you to do something, go somewhere, or be included in an upcoming event. There are wedding invitations and surprise party invitations; invitations to dinner or a graduation, an invitation to a friend's house or an invitation to go fishing. Each one is asking you to make a choice. To go or not to go, to participate or not to participate, to be present or be absent...you choose...always!

If you are excited about accepting the invitation, then there is enthusiasm on your part to do what the invitation requests. An invitation to something that looks like great fun creates a sense of joy and anticipation and you just can't wait for the day to arrive.

Being responsible for yourself means that you are, and always have been, in charge. Everything is a choice and you are the one choosing. Your unhealthy habits and addictions are not running the show, although sometimes we might find ourselves saying things like: "I have such a habit of being late, I'll never make it," "I'll never lose the weight to look good enough to go to that reunion." "I can't stand the way I look." "My addiction is just out of control." Or "My addiction is raging and just won't quit." Those statements turn your unhealthy habits and addictions into tangible, conscious things, capable of making their own decisions. Those demeaning statements attribute more responsibility, more power, and more credit to your unhealthy behaviors and addictions than they actually have or deserve. All of that inner dialogue and gremlin chatter can make you feel separate from yourself.

As you come to know and Love YOU, you can consider the thought that you are always the one making the decisions. By inviting yourself to be responsible for your life, you eliminate any excuses to fail to make healthy choices for your own well-being. Decide to make the invitation failsafe by using compassion and kindness to offer the choice. Make the party attractive enough so that every part of you wants to join the celebration; especially your sober healthy self.

Love Your Sensitive Self

Fifteen Ways to Practice Grace in Your Life

Are you a sensitive person? Have you ever had people say things like: "You are just too sensitive." "Do you have to be so sensitive?" "Can't you take a joke...?" "I was just kidding." "Chill out, and don't be so offended." "You get too upset at the little things." "Don't be so sensitive."

Little did you realize, but being sensitive is the juice of living a peaceful and graceful life. Being sensitive is an asset when you know how to use it. The skill of being sensitive is being cultivated for your best interest and for the good of all around you.

At its best, when you are sensitive to someone being rude or disrespectful, you can make a choice to recognize that not only are you just as capable of being mean, but that you would make a conscious decision to *not* be rude or disrespectful to someone else.

You are making the choice to be different and to not engage in hurtful behaviors.

It would be very easy to be or do the things that you see happening around you. It doesn't take much to act rude or critical towards others. Possibly having an attitude of being mindful and aware of others will help you hold onto the idea that we are all connected in some way. This human adventure is certainly a challenge, but with healthy decisions, this life experience can be joyous and loving. When we wake up to the truth that we always have a choice in how we respond and act, we gain a sense of courage which gives us the power to change things and make them better.

As you begin to become comfortable in your own skin, you will notice that life becomes vivid and vibrant. If you are a sensitive person, you will become aware of your own sensitivity to everything.... I mean *everything*. You will hear better, see more, notice little details, react with genuine feeling and emotion, and trust your growing intuition.

To cultivate sensitivity and live a life of grace:

1. Start by making friends with your breath. Practice being conscious when you inhale and exhale, and even say to yourself, "I am breathing in, and I am breathing out."

2. Learn to slow down.

3. Suspend judgment.

4. Investigate motivation and realize people do things for two reasons: either for love or for fear. When there is fear, there is a need for more love and when there is love, there can be no fear.

5. When you are afraid, put your hand on your heart and listen to your inner wisdom.

6. Trust your intuition.

7. Exercise your intuition.

8. Learn to become your own best friend.

9. Be gentle with personal expectations and with expectations of others.

10. Know in your very bones that all human beings want to be happy. Some of them do a better job than others of actually practicing the choice of happiness.

11. Practice forgiveness; when you forgive, you actually give up the idea of a better past.

12. Spend at least ten minutest out in nature daily and notice everything...the sky, the clouds, the wind, the butterflies, the sounds, the smells, the grass, the street, the birds, the air, or the wind.

13. Celebrate when you are being sensitive to others, to Mother Earth, and to yourself.

14. Practice opening your heart. Actually imagine that your heart is an open flame of loving kindness and that it radiates from the middle of your chest.

15. Gracefully walk through your life with joy, peace, and ease as your companions.

Letting Go to Love YOU or How Best to Enjoy a Roller Coaster

Sam took many years to come to a place where he was willing to put genuine effort into making healthy choices. He committed himself to a variety of programs and therapies until one day, at an amusement park, he experienced an "a-ha" moment of personal truth. He was on a quest to fall in love with himself and doing the behaviors which supported healthy choices for his life. His wisdom is an interesting metaphor surrendering into love.

"One of the hardest things to do is to manage our own lives. It takes so much work, planning, provisions, damage control, net moves. Not to mention the innumerable fears associated with wondering how each move will turn out. It's stressful just to think

about everything involved.

"Fortunately, there is an alternative; a softer way: letting go and letting God. Or letting go and letting the Universe. Letting go is analogous to the moment when we crest the top of the roller coaster climb. On the way up it's tick-tick-tick, and we're eager with anticipation for the thrill. As soon as the clicking stops and we start the ride in earnest, the best way to enjoy it is simply to let go and trust that it'll be fun. If we let fear consume us, if we grip the sides of the car, if we worry whether it'll hold on the tracks, if we're fearful we may barf up a hot dog or worse, then we kiss the fun goodbye. Which way sounds more loving? Surrender and let go so you can learn to love your healthy sober self!"

Chapter 12

Wiggle Your Toes and Land in Your Body

We have come to a point in our evolution where we spend most of our time in our heads. We are just thinking too much and we rarely pay attention to the wisdom that is available to us from our bodies.

As human beings, we are usually preoccupied about our thinking and rarely do we settle into our bodies for information. Coming to know your body might be a delightful adventure. It could be the most amazing wonderland you have ever experienced. That is, if you are willing to practice the strategies necessary to getting yourself there.

The growing research about body wisdom is encouraging, freeing, and inviting. Your body is the chamber that houses your very essence. Your body is the vehicle that carries you around in the world. Your body is the uniform that marches your soul along the road of life. Your body holds your truth and all your stories. Your body stays with you until your last breath leaves and you die and pass to another realm of consciousness. You only get one body in this lifetime and it is eager to play in the game of living. Your body knows everything and is ready to guide you towards healthy decisions.

There is language we use that indicates that we already know about body wisdom, even if we are still learning to harness the power of hearing what our bodies say. Have you ever heard statements like: "I can just feel it in my bones." "That made my skin crawl." "The hair on the back of my neck is standing up." "I just got a rush of goose bumps." "My stomach is in knots." "My head is about to explode." "My hands are tingling." "My throat is closing up." "I have a weight on my chest," "My heart is broken," "He spilled his guts on the table" "I am keeping an eye on you." "You make my heart sing."

People use their bodies for feedback and have really no idea how accurate, how insightful, and how important the information is to them.

Wiggling your toes is a small technique to help you "land in your body" and feel present. There is a heaviness of settling into your skin, which will soon become familiar. Think of the process of being in your body as simply coming home; arriving at the station, entering your vehicle of existence, becoming aware of your space, being born again with every breath. The following "Love Your Solid Self" section has some ideas to welcome you home to the glorious body that holds your precious self.

Love Your Solid Self

Eight Ways to be solid in your body

When you are hurting, being in your body is not the easiest thing to make happen. Much of the time, we are floating in our heads and it is only when pain stings either emotionally, physically, or even spiritually, that we might momentarily experience a physical encounter with ourselves.

The truth about being human and the trick to staying healthy and sober is simply to listen to your body and learn the language of muscular tissue and cell dialogue. You were born into a body that has always known the truth—that you are precious, unique, and pure love—regardless of what has happened, is happening, or might happen to you in the future.

It does take courage to stay present and learn to be in your body." These statements can help: "Take a deep breath and drop into your body." "Land in your body." "Sense your body." "Feel your body." "Listen to your body." "Feel grounded or solid." "Touch the earth." "Intuitively know yourself." "Be in touch with your body."

How do you know? Who will see you in your body and give you the feedback that, indeed, you are there, especially if you have not been there lately? Here are some tips to help you do just that; be in your body and be solid about being present.

1. Take deep breaths as often as you remember.

2. Consciously think about your breathing and feel the air enter your nose or mouth as you inhale and notice the warmth of the air as you exhale.

3. Imagine that you—the you who is reading this—is intentionally thinking about being in your body and bring your attention to your left big toe. Notice what might be going on there.

4. Experience a body scan by bringing your attention to each part of your body independently and slowly, one part at a time. You can find a free audio description of a body scan used by the program Mindfulness Based Relapse Preventi (MBRP) on the Internet at mindfulrp.com or search for a body scan on YouTube.

5. Slow down...way down...walk slowly, talk slowly, look carefully, and move slowly. Try it every day for a few minutes. While you are going to your car, brushing your teeth, eating a meal; be mindful.

6. Sit still, find a comfortable position, and imagine you are filling yourself up from the inside out. All of you is coming out of your head and pouring into your body.

7. Let yourself sit for a few minutes (or longer), sensing the heaviness of being in your body. Scan the solid sensation by using your imagination and declaring it to be so. You can say: "I am present in my body right now."

8. Sense a heaviness in your arms and legs. Feel thick and solid in your skin. Fill yourself up with your own magnificence and top it off with a smile.

David was having a heck of a time "landing in his body." The traumas of his past and his addiction to drugs, alcohol, and gambling were haunting his willingness to find time to feel his body and accept that loving himself was his ever-present challenge.

One night, while struggling with the process of a body scan, he decided to take a warm bubble bath. Sure, he thought it was a little weird to take a bubble bath in order to give himself permission to be in his body.

According to David, "It worked, and felt great!"

Michael's Take on Pain's Silver Lining

"I've been on many diets in my life, and one thing I've discovered is that one or two days into them, I typically experience hunger pangs, a subset of pain in general. While these pangs aren't exactly pleasant, I've learned to look forward to them. Why? Because in the vein of "no-pain-no-gain," they serve as a measuring stick, or barometer that the diet is working. The trick, of course, is not to soothe the pain by scarfing down four or five bowls of Frosted Flakes, but to know that the pangs will pass, and, as a direct result, I'll be a happier camper when I next step on the scale.

"Similarly, as a teacher of math, I am quite familiar with the intellectual pain that learning new mathematical material causes students. I tell my students to look forward to that pain, as it's a sure sign of engaging with new and challenging stuff; a sure sign of learning. If they can bear with a certain amount of discomfort, perhaps even anxiety, while their brains are connecting new material to old, they'll inevitably get through to the other side of understanding. In a month, they'll look back and wonder why they put themselves through so much pain over material that now seems so transparent.

"Recently, I've been dealing with anger and resentment towards family members and colleagues and bosses along my path to making healthy choices and choosing sobriety. Whether my feelings are justified or not, I know that anger and resentment do me a lot more harm than good, regardless of the specifics. Consequently, I want to surrender enough to trust the process. That however, does not, (at least in the short run) necessarily dissipate the pain that underlies anger and resentment. For me, it still comes out, often sideways. What I recently and quite suddenly realized is that that's OK. Just as hunger pangs are a barometer of the efficacy of a diet, and just as mathematical frustration is a barometer of the learning curve, so too are the pain and sometimes sideways expressions of anger barometers of growth in recovery. If we stay the course, the pain goes away

and, lo, we lose the weight, learn the material, and move past our resentment. The short-term pain is, in this light, not a dark cloud, but rather a silver lining that illuminates a path towards loving ourselves."

Chapter 13

Minimize the Shame Icon Running in the Background

To feel guilty is to feel regretful and remorseful for a wrongdoing. When you feel guilty, you can often rectify the action. If you break a window with a flying baseball, you find a way to replace the window. But to feel shameful is to have a sense of personal disgrace, dishonor, and to be ashamed of who you are as a human being. In unhealthy habits, destructive behaviors, and addictive cycles, shame rises relentlessly before, during, and after engaging in the behaviors that keep you distant from health, well-being, and sobriety.

We continue to struggle with this basic emotion. In today's world, we have not yet given ourselves permission to even talk about shame. Feeling shameful initiates a desire to cover up the activity, the feelings, even the consequences, and avoid responsibility at all costs. Feeling shameful is directly linked to lying and avoiding the truth of what is happening to you.

Would you feel shameful if you were: Spending some of the household savings on a sure bet at the track, taking advantage of a friend's generosity, buying extra snacks and eating them before you get home, secretly holding onto an email address without telling your partner, hiding the credit card bills, locking the bathroom door to take additional pills, hiding the pot you just scored, or even exploding with anger and rage towards someone you dearly love?

Here, a couple struggles with their emotional addiction to anger and rage. The pain impacts the entire family and shame underscores the road to recovery.

> *Bonnie and Cory had two children, Michael, age six, and Wendy, age eight. As parents, their personalities were oil and water, and they never missed an opportunity to be sarcastic and cutting with each other. Their banter was an old habit of early courtship, and it carried over into the marriage.*

> *The trouble started when the couple began fighting in front of the children and just couldn't seem to stop themselves. Having lost their emotional connection to each other, they also lost their ability to understand the consequences of the rage-filled, angry behavior.*

> *When their daughter began having violent outbursts and uncontrollable temper tantrums, the energy in the home spun out of control. Screaming matches, power struggles and finally violent hitting brought both parents into therapy. Their addiction to anger and rage had created a fearful environment for the entire family. Embarrassment and shame eroded their emotional stability as a couple. They were terrified of what they were modeling for their children.*

Shame carries with it the memories of past judgments and criticism and keeps you captive when present-day behavior just doesn't measure up to either your own expectations or those of others in your life.

The hope for recovery and learning to Love YOU happens when we cradle our shame with compassion and understanding. Only then can we begin to heal the dark entanglement from tears of humiliation, and the red-hot burn of embarrassment.

Shame, as well as health and sobriety, are running in the background of your life. We have all been exposed to the toxic emotion of shame, and have felt the burning of worthlessness etched into our very souls. There are marks all over our lives made by others who might have wagged a finger and shouted, "shame on you!" Humiliation, dishonor, and inadequacy are key players in perpetrating the pain of shame.

When shame takes over, you could crumble and dissolve figuratively, and sometimes physically, into unhealthy habits and often times addictive behaviors. Overwhelming feelings of helplessness and hopelessness could leave you with an urge to *do something*. The emotional pain creeps in slowly, or sometimes arrives even at lightning speed, and leaves you raw, vulnerable, unconscious, and ready to act out and make unhealthy choices that might seem automatic.

Knowledge is power and Socrates was right: "Know thyself" was his guiding rule, and by coming to know and understand yourself, lifetime joy will always be available to you if you so choose.

Since you are coming to know your healthy, vibrant, sober self, and learning how to become your own best friend, you can master many things by simply naming your feelings, claiming your feelings, and finally, taming your feelings. In short: name it, claim it, and tame it. Rather than being so hard on yourself and denying the authentic parts of you, you will come to stand by yourself, show up with a tender, friendly gesture of love for all your feelings, even shame. And when you do, you will be able to have your true feelings work for you, rather than against you.

Shame can be healed with sympathetic concern and empathy. Most important, it is compassion for yourself and a genuine sense of empathy for all that you have endured up until this very day.

Why not replace the shame icon running in the background of your life, first with self-forgiveness and then with the icon of *Loving YOU*. It is *your* life and *your* programming and *you* get to design your life in any way that works for you. With a single click, health and sobriety can take over the screen and remind you what is important and what your priorities are. You are developing the tools to regroup, reorganize, and reinvent yourself in the midst of difficult decisions.

Think of your thoughts, feelings, and emotions as chemical ingredients landing in your brain and in your body. All of those elements swimming around remind me of an old story called "Stone Soup." A poor farmer's wife had nothing to eat and decided that she would convince her neighbors that she was making a delicious stone soup and they could share in the feast if they each brought just one ingredient. All she had was a stone, water and the fire beneath the caldron. All the neighbors were excited, because her faith and belief in the soup was undeniably inspiring. Guests added potatoes, carrots, celery root, kale, garlic, onions, beets, spinach, sweet potatoes, squash, beans, herbs and spices. The soup started out with a stone, but the good ingredients are what made the difference.

When you have a choice, bring in the positive ingredients for a delicious soup of life. A best friend would do that for you in a heartbeat. (Again the body shows up...in a heartbeat!) Why not do it for yourself and choose carefully and with deliberate action in order to create a healthy, prosperous, and joyous experience to call your own?

Love Your Shameful Self

How to Use Your Beautiful Heart to Ease Your Life

Keep this in mind: The Health of the Mind is in direct proportion to the Gratitude of the Heart. HeartMath research supports the concept that gratitude and appreciation change the physiology of our emotional soup. HeartMath teaches resilience, how to reduce stress, techniques to

self-regulate emotions, and even helps you experience better sleep. There are more electrical currents going from the
heart to the brain than from the brain to the heart. Our intelligence is grounded in the heart and it is finally time to
recognize this power.

The Heart-Lock-In Tool is a strategy for well-being and
is easily integrated into your day.... Practice is the key.

Here's a reminder to make your goodness shine
through as you inspire the love muscle within your own
self.

1. Shift your attention to the area of your heart and
    breathe slowly and deeply.

2. Activate and sustain genuine feelings of apprecia-
    tion or care for someone or something in your life.

3. Send these feelings of care towards yourself and
    then to others (this benefits them and especially
    helps recharge and balance your own energies).

4. When you catch your mind wandering, refocus to
    your heart and reconnect with the feelings of care
    and appreciation. Repeat as often as you remem-
    ber. See http://www.heartmath.com for more in-
    formation.

Chapter 14

Mind Dialogue: You Are the One Talking in the First Place

If the gremlins and the committee in your head are not necessarily running the show, then who is really ordering lunch?

You might often feel as though there are a number of voices chatting in your mind and making no sense at all. They say things like, "You should do this." "No, try this way." "You don't know what you are doing." "Better not try that idea." "Wait, I have an idea." "Can you imagine what she must be thinking?" "Don't even think you can make that happen." "Who do you think you are?" "Better think again, that won't work." "I never will get this right."

What you say to yourself is exactly what you will get! Being critical of yourself or others, doubting a healthy decision, judging an action or others, creating a risky scenario, replaying a conversation, unwinding an event, all of these are thoughts that run the show without your input.

Imagine the thoughts in your mind as the words in the script of your life. The interesting thing is that you can rewrite the dialogue at any time.

Awareness is the first step in understanding the power you have over your inner dialogue. Stop long enough to hear what you are saying to yourself. Take stock and analyze the negative and judgmental comments that run through your head on a continual basis and begin to ask those thoughts to wait until another time. Rather than erasing them and finding yourself in an internal struggle of power and control, just say, "Not now," when a negative, judgmental or critical thought shows up. Learn to replace the negative with a more positive and promising thought. Create thoughts of:

- Optimism: "I know I can figure this out."

- Simplicity: "Life is getting easier and I can make this decision simple."

- Trust: "I trust that I can learn to make healthy decisions for my success."

- Positivity: "Intuitively I know what is best for my well-being."

- Forgiveness: "My heart is learning to forgive myself and others."

- Action: "I make things happen for my health and for the good of others."

- Grace: "It is easy for me to be loving to myself and others."

You can design your own list of attributes that will support the Love YOU intention.

Love Your Sincere Self

Ten Truths to Live By

Sincerity means to be free from pretense and deceit. When you are sincere, you are genuine in how you feel and what you believe; not dishonest or hypocritical. Living by the truth is a choice and a challenge. Being honest with yourself and trusting your inner knowing might be new and a bit strange. Your body knows when the truth is out of alignment, almost like a built-in lie detector. You can deny things all you want, but sooner or later the truth will reveal itself.

"The truth will set you free" is a statement many of us have heard, but never understood. Here are a few ways to reflect on what it means:

♦ Be a compassionate witness to your own story.

♦ The past is over and your power is in the present moment.

♦ Practice forgiveness.

♦ Cultivate your intuition and trust it.

♦ Learn to be gentle with yourself.

♦ Slow down.

- Make your integrity visible to yourself and to others.

- Build credibility, character, and competence.

- Live with a grateful heart 24/7.

- Become an enlightened witness to your own life and then to the lives of others.

Katherine is coming to know her healthy, sober self and delights in the moments that reinforce the commitment she has towards herself and her sobriety.

"I have a beautiful four-year-old granddaughter, Sadie, that I call Muffy (she's my rag-a-muffin). At Thanksgiving her pre-school teacher asked the kids what they were grateful for, and each child said their mom or a sibling. When she asked Sadie, she exclaimed: "I'm grateful for my Nana." I was on the top of the world. When I think it would be nice to have a glass of wine, I remember what that beautiful four-year-old said about me. And I realize that I am in love with my healthy sober self."

Chapter 15

Tricks to Pull One Over on Your Own Brain

Stop for a moment. Wherever you are, just stop and put your hand over your heart and be very still. Feel your chest rise and fall with the inhalation and exhalation of your breathing. Imagine a warm light expanding from your heart and radiating throughout your body. Connect the light from your heart to the light in your brain with an intention of care and compassion. Allow yourself a moment of calm and notice how you feel in your body. Your ability to conjure up inner connections of energy is a powerful technique; simple, easy, and always available.

When we orchestrate that internal energy with purpose and direction, electrical currents charge positive forces that support our health and well-being.

The trick is to do this exercise often and whenever you are not sure of what to do next. Giving your heart and brain time to connect will offer you the wisdom you need to make healthy choices in your life, and will help you celebrate Loving You.

As mentioned before, *HeartMath* has shown us that the energy being emitted by the heart is far more powerful than the energy coming from the brain. The ancient Egyptians had it right. They honored the heart first, and declared that all human wisdom was held in the heart rather than in the brain. The heart was viewed as the source of emotions, memory, personality, the spirit, and even the soul of mankind.

Coming to know your heart and your brain and learning to work in concert with your inner wisdom will give you the courage to design action towards health and well-being.

The habits of thinking are steeped in deep patterns formed from your past Your brain and your mind will not give in easily.... Tell them both that you have made friends with your heart and intend to include it from now on. Decide to form a friendship between you, your mind, and your heart that lives up to the idea of "all for one, and one for all." You, your heart, and your brain, like the three musketeers, come together to protect, defend, and celebrate your one and only healthy and sober self.

Love Your Stubborn, Stormy Self

Ten Ways to Wait Out the Storms in Your Heart

Let me share with you an incident that brings to mind the importance of patience. I was working on my computer late one night and was almost oblivious to the weather happening right outside my window. About midnight, a horrifying rainstorm blew through the area with no warning and grabbed my attention.

In less than an hour, trees and power lines dropped like leaves falling to the ground. When the lights went out and the computer went dead, I was sure I was in was Kansas, in the middle of Dorothy's tornado. Destruction happened quickly and without warning. There was a whirlwind of debris all over the neighborhood. In the morning light and the calm of the next day, I was able to assess the damage and put things back in balance. In the heat of the fury, I could only wait for the storm to pass before I could make things right.

Have you had the experience of an emotional storm rise inside you, without warning, and throw you off-center? In that emotional fury, did you choose to express the energy as an angry outburst, a disappointing encounter, an irritating look, a frustrating conversation, an annoying attitude, or even a violent attack? If you wait for the storm to pass— just wait it out—the emotional energy will move *through* you rather than *using* you to damage those around you; often those you love and cherish the most.

1.   Linger in a place of patience.

2.   Slow down; trust your breath and the present moment to ground you.

3.   Think of something or someone you love.

4.   Remind yourself of the gratitude you have been practicing.

5. Remember that forgiveness is a gift you give yourself.

6. Wait, wait, wait...and wait some more.

7. Keep breathing in and out, in and out.

8. Say out loud to yourself: "This too shall pass, this too shall pass."

9. Practice compassion for yourself, the situation, and others.

10. Tell yourself that everything, everything is a choice.

Remember, as we discussed earlier, the mind creates thoughts and sometimes those thoughts are indeed a little or a lot hysterically crazy. You may not have control over the first thought your mind creates, but you do have control over how you react and respond to that thought. You always have a choice over your behavior and response.

There is a calm after the storm, and when the energy passes, your thinking will clear, your attitude will become kind, your heart will open, and you will make a different choice of thought, pattern, and behavior.

There will be far less mess to clean up in the morning. In practicing to Love YOU, you are practicing the self-love you are learning when you remember to be your own best friend.

Chapter 16

Stop Seeking Experts and Start Living Your Life

It is a waste of time to think that someone else knows you better than you do. It is fine to collect opinions and suggestions from people who care about your welfare, but to be honest, only you can do anything about it. While you are checking out the experts, reading their latest self-help books, attending lectures and listening to podcasts, reviewing articles and searching for answers, you are delaying the action that just might save your life.

All of the answers to all of your questions, and all of your problems for that matter, are already inside you. Having the ability to listen and actually *hear* that information comes with the ability to fall in love with yourself.

Think of collective wisdom as the necessary and vital part of upgrading and improving your access to information in order to improve your life. Similar to your computer, the ongoing downloads arrive just in time to improve your programing. You select the option to upgrade because the intelligence in cyberspace and the powers that be have suggested that your equipment will function better with the new software.

You have continual and perpetual access to all the wisdom in the universe if you would simply plug yourself into the self-love that is always waiting on the sidelines. You don't need approval from anyone to start living the life you want. The only thing you must do is *choose* to put behaviors in place by creating actions that will ensure success.

You are the one in charge of your life. Simply make the decision to change and then develop a plan. Find others to support your healthy decisions, and then go about working your plan. Remember to celebrate your successes and accept yourself unconditionally.

This story offers hope and encouragement that loving who you are first is a solid prescription for health, well-being, and sobriety.

Marilyn, now in her forties, has seven years of sobriety under her belt. Love YOU was a new feeling for her and she realized that she was no longer seeking approval from others. The glory of being sober was hers and hers alone, and she was grateful. Staying sober was no longer the terrifying struggle she experienced in the beginning of her recovery. She wasn't counting and remembering the last time she picked up a drink or engaged in drug use. Instead, she was comfortably living a sober life and loving it.

Marilyn learned to trust her inner self because she had developed a love affair with herself and an appreciation for her ability to make healthy choices. She was no longer seeking advice from experts, but was living her life in a healthy, positive, and flourishing manner.

Honoring your "Solo Self," will help you trust that you do have what it takes to make healthy choices when you love yourself first.

Love Your Solo Self

Twelve ways to honor your preciousness

There is often a feeling of panic and abandonment at the thought of "giving up" your habits, unhealthy behaviors, and addictions; even when it becomes apparent that it is necessary for your health and well-being.

You might even think of your old unhealthy habit as a very close friend, someone you have spent many years with and have loved dearly. That friend is always calling you and asking you to do something for them. Sometimes you have to go out of your way to help that friend and sometimes it feels as if they are taking advantage of you. You never cared much that your friend was usually busy or preoccupied when you needed their help. You were always so very understanding and that friend was grateful that you made it all OK.

It didn't matter that your friend couldn't help you, or had a myriad of excuses when you needed them. Maybe they just didn't have the energy or the time to give to you, but you didn't care because you thought that love was enough. You always, always saw their better side. Other friends might have even tried to tell you that you were being exploited and that it was not fair for you to be the one always making the sacrifices and the compromises.

Think of your unhealthy habits and harmful addictions as old friends who never really gave anything to the relationship.

Truthfully, your unhealthy habit or even your drug of choice, whether it was alcohol, cocaine, pot, gambling, sex, sugar, food, the internet, love and relationships, working, performance, perfection, eating, texting, sexing, fighting, negative thinking, swearing, excising, TV, or gaming, was your best friend and sometimes has been your life-long buddy. However, it has been a one-sided relationship. The only thing you could rely on was the consistency of engaging in your unhealthy habits or your addiction to numb any uncomfortable feelings of loneliness, sadness, or even fear, and postpone any authentic activity of honest desire to be present in life.

Being alone has perhaps been a very unsettling feeling for you. As human beings, we are programed to be together. It is in our DNA, and companionship and community are close to our sense of belonging.

Your unhealthy habits and addiction have been in charge and you just might be tired. Perhaps you are thinking that if you change your behavior to the healthy choice, you will be more than alone; you will be shunned by others and left to wallow in your own self-pity. No one will like you anymore because you won't be any fun, and if you are healthy and sober, you will be too scared to even be around people. No longer having your unhealthy habits and addictions to hide behind or walk with will leave you naked and isolated from friends and family. You dread having to decline a drink, or a cupcake, or even a trip to the local bar.

Think of it as saying goodbye to that friend who just couldn't be there to help when you needed support. Tell yourself you are flying solo for a while, just to see how it feels.

You are learning to live your life as a healthy and sober human being, doing the best you can to be happy. Your mission is to become your own best friend and fill that relationship with love, compassion, forgiveness, and tenderness.

Twelve Ways to Love Your Solo Self

1. Greet yourself enthusiastically every morning. Look in the mirror, wink at yourself and say "Glad to have you back."

2. Buy yourself a new toothbrush every other month in the color of your choice. It's personal, inexpensive, and just for you. It also helps improve your dental hygiene.

3. Buy flowers for yourself and display them where you can enjoy them.

4. Take yourself to the movies, theater, or concerts on occasion.

5. Smile while you are getting dressed. You might have to fake it for a while, but the pleasant brain chemicals will help you feel better about being you.

6. Create a gratitude list. Every night list at least ten things you are grateful for and make them different every night.

7. Read your gratitude list in the morning and add anything you would like.

8. Shower regularly, wash your hair, buy scented soap, use deodorant, take more baths, and learn to love and care for your body.

9. Eat well; fruits and veggies, vitamins and protein. Drink more water.

10. Put your left hand on your right shoulder and your right hand on your left shoulder and hug yourself at least three times a day.

11. Place your hand over your heart whenever you think about it. Feel your heart beat, notice your breathing and relish in the warmth of your own love.

12. Just decide (yes'm! it's a choice!) to love yourself unconditionally.

Chapter 17

Pocket Your Own Best Friend...YOU!

Throughout this little book, you have been asked to Love YOU and different parts of yourself. Now it is time for you to just love your entire self and learn to become your own best friend. It doesn't matter if you have had a bad experience with a best friend, if you never had a best friend, or if you don't even want a best friend. To ensure a healthy, happy, and sober life, you will flourish and be joyful as you learn to become your own best friend.

When you come to love yourself without conditions and with an open heart, you are elegantly poised to engage in a genuine and loving friendship with yourself.

Honoring who you are and respecting yourself is an easy place to start. If you are someone who is constantly criticizing and judging yourself, it is time to stop and redesign your thinking. Personal respect and compassion play a major role in developing friendship, not only with others, but more importantly, with yourself. Honoring your boundaries and expectations helps to keep you aware of what is happening around you. Playing the role of a wonderful, nurturing, loving, and devoted parent to yourself gives you the encouragement and guidance to learn more about how to act towards yourself and towards others.

Practice forgiveness. Acquire the skills of forgiveness and start with yourself. You know how to be a best friend, so get over it and do that for yourself.

The literary geniuses of our time have put forth the value of a best friend, and as you glance through the quotes, in the deepest part of your heart, know and see yourself as your own best friend. Take stock of how you feel at the end of the quotes:

- Yesterday brought the beginning, tomorrow brings the end, and somewhere in the middle we became the best of friends. ~Author Unknown

- A friend is the one who comes in when the whole world has gone out. ~Grace Pulpit

- A true friend is one who thinks you are a good egg even if you are half-cracked. ~Author Unknown

- What is a friend? A single soul dwelling in two bodies. ~Aristotle

- A friend can tell you things you don't want to tell yourself. ~Frances Ward Weller

- A friend accepts us as we are yet helps us to be what we should. ~Author Unknown

- Only your real friends will tell you when your face is dirty. ~Sicilian Proverb

- The language of friendship is not words but meanings. ~Henry David Thoreau

- The bird a nest, the spider a web, man friendship. ~William Blake

- It is one of the blessings of old friends that you can afford to be stupid with them. ~Ralph Waldo Emerson

- Ah, how good it feels! The hand of an old friend. ~Henry Wadsworth Longfellow

- I felt it shelter to speak to you. ~Emily Dickinson

- Promise you won't forget me, because if I thought you would, I'd never leave. ~Winnie the Pooh

- A real friend is one who walks in when the rest of the world walks out. ~Walter Winchell

- A true friend is someone who knows there's something wrong even when you have the biggest smile on your face. Walking with a friend in the dark is better than walking alone in the light. ~Helen Keller

- Think about being: Braver that you are, Stronger than you seem, Smarter than you think. ~Mary Pope Osborne

Finding the strength and courage to become your own best friend begins with a choice and a commitment. Here, in the following wisdom, are some tips in polishing up your Shinning Self.

Love Your Shinning Self

Seven Steps to polish the glow from within

Here are seven steps to help you create a glow from within:

1. Shift your awareness to the area around your heart.

2. Breathe as if your heart were your lungs.

3. Imagine a shining, bright light coming from your heart area.

4. Watch your breath as it comes in and out of your heart and lights up the brightness within.

5. Listen to the wisdom your heart has to share. Don't edit it in your head; just listen to what comes up into your imagination and stay with the feelings.

6. Trust that your inner light and precious essence is always shinning, you just have to train yourself to notice.

7. Allow the light to wash over you and soften as you feel the compassion and care that you are cultivating for yourself.

Chapter 18

Straight Talk for the Scaffolding Required

In the world of education, "scaffolding" is the new term used to identify the temporary help and guidance a child receives when learning new skills. Scaffolding represents a temporary framework that supports the learning and skill building until successful independence is achieved.

Helping a toddler learn to walk by holding her hand and encouraging new steps leads to watching her run in a million directions. Reading to a preschooler to improve his language skills results in his confidence, curiosity, and a love of reading. Teaching a teenager to drive and make reasonable and wise decisions ensures the roads will be safer with a future responsible driver.

Scaffolding support can come in many forms. Traditionally, scaffolding is used by workers to help them build, repair, or clean a high structure like a building or a cathedral. You might see scaffolding made of wooden planks and poles, which support the artists bringing a facelift to the structure, but doesn't obstruct the view.

The scaffolding created for a child's learning can also come in a variety of forms. The learning scaffolding is set up to encourage independence and challenge, but not to over-shadow the ability to perform the task. A youngster doesn't want wooden planks and poles, but will gladly take oral coaching, demonstrations, outlines, models of appropriate answers, story descriptions, case histories, real-life illustra-tions, flash cards, key questions, outlines, side notes, props, cues, guided practice, reference materials, cheat sheets, review quizzes, practice runs, think-aloud problem solving, and so on.

The scaffolding, either in a child's learning or in learn-ing to Love YOU, is temporary. You can, however, keep it around until you have integrated the skills of loving your-self and until your well-being and sobriety support a healthy lifestyle.

For example, Alcoholics Anonymous sets up the scaf-folding for recovery as a sponsor, the 12 steps, a fellowship to feel a part of, speaker meetings, *Big Book* meetings, home groups, and more. Weight Watchers offers community, meetings, and now even online coaching.

You know what you need and will learn to design your own personal scaffolding. As you come to understand the paramount importance for the fail-safe support you set up for yourself, you will ensure success in your search for health and sobriety. Action always makes a difference, and you are shopping for the action to ensure that the love you have for yourself will prevail.

As you fall in love with your healthy and sober self, you will develop the ability to design a plan of action, orchestrate that plan, and then evaluate the results. Many of these skills might be new at this point in your life. Let's face it; in the past you have usually found yourself at the bottom of a plan you never intended on implementing and then picking up your "sorry self" in order to start all over again.

While designing a plan of action, ask: "What prior information do I need to think about?" "Why am I doing this; what is my payoff?" "What should I do first?" "What have the consequences been in the past?" "What can I expect to happen?"

During the plan of action, ask: "How am I doing right now?" "Is this where I want to be?" "What can I remember for next time?" "Should I change anything right now?" "What do I need to do if this is not working?"

After the plan of action, ask: "How well did I do?" "Did my plan work in my best interests?" "What could I have done differently?" "Do I need to learn something new?" "Can I apply what I learned to future decisions?"

You can't build a cathedral without scaffolding, so what makes you think you can maintain a healthy life without support?

New brain research indicates we were not meant to live alone. Your tribe and community are vital to your health and well-being. How do you develop a support network? You will become the expert in your life and will know intuitively what to do next. You do not have to do this alone. The more scaffolding you create for yourself, the more fun you will have living your life as a healthy, sober, creative, and loving individual.

This is a marathon race and sprinting is only a piece of the excitement. Choose from the ideas in how to "Love Your Sprinting Self" and make healthy choices that will ensure fewer problems and new skills for happiness.

Love Your Sprinting Self

Twenty Ways to Win Long-Distance Living

Life sometimes feels like a marathon; you are in this race for the long haul. You must keep moving because everything is constantly changing. In a real long-distance race, where you have to run for five miles or more, you wouldn't enter the race without being physically, emotionally, and psychologically ready.

On the other hand, sprinting is a different kind of race and demands a tremendous amount of energy over a very short period of time. Both types of races—the marathon and the sprint—often leave you exhausted at the finish line.

If you are sprinting in your life, that is, running from event to event, pushing deadlines from project to project, scheduling meeting after meeting, taking phone calls into the night, missing family time because of commitments, neglecting to have some genuine fun and relaxation, and never taking time to be still, you are putting yourself and your well-being at risk. You are not only missing out on the joys of life, but you are also turning off your ability to hook into a natural source of support.

Give yourself permission to rest, slow down, unplug, watch, reflect, and notice the opportunities available to you. We don't always have to *do*; sometimes we need to just *be*. You really don't want to get to the Heavenly Gates and tell St. Peter that you wished you had worked more during your life. Most people would agree that at the end of life, their only regret would be "could I have loved more and enjoyed living fully and with joy." Everything in life is a choice.

How Will You Choose?

1. Start your day by saying: "There is nothing that I *have* to do." And "I have my whole lifetime to do it."

2. Stop, look, and listen when you get up from your desk at work to walk to the bathroom, kitchen, or to get the mail.

3. Sit for a moment in the morning and watch yourself breathe...in and out for at least five breaths.

4. When you first wake up, take three deep breaths and tell yourself that today you will find joy.

5. Study mindfulness and practice it every day.

6. Learn to meditate and practice every day.

7. Find a hobby and begin to invest in quality time for your own personal enjoyment.

8. Ask yourself, "What is the most loving thing I can do for myself right now?"

9. Listen with your heart to the people in your world and to yourself. Ask yourself, "What do I need right now" and listen to your heart for the answer.

10. Watch and play with kids.

11. Listen to nature. Spend time in it.

12. Walk outside under the sky for at least thirty minutes a day.

13. Incorporate a fifty-minute work hour. Work for only fifty minutes and take ten minutes to do something entirely different.

14. Brew fresh tea and give yourself permission to enjoy the entire cup.

15. Take a deep breath every time you come to a red light.

16. Take power naps.

17. Listen to your favorite music.

18. Keep an inspirational magazine in your car and browse through it during traffic jams.

19. Be a passenger and watch out the window.

20. Go to bed, but go to bed earlier.

Chapter 19

Watch Out for Dirty Glasses on the Nightstand

There has to be a place for us to talk about slipping up, falling off the wagon, using, missing the mark, picking up, losing the game, giving in....

When you are not loving yourself, especially your healthy, sober self, you begin to convince yourself that you are different and that unhealthy choices are really OK in your world.

What gives you the confidence to give yourself permission to slip up? Ever considered the thinking behind your choices? How about simply the action of basic Human Nature? That's right. You are human, and after a certain length of time and given a certain amount of stress, under certain circumstances, you just might stop paying attention to yourself and you might slip up.

Moving your world from unhealthy to healthy is a major accomplishment.

Your willingness to stay awake and stay vigilant to your decisions is an ongoing challenge. Healthy decisions = fewer problems. A very powerful mantra.

Take stock of your life, your living experience, your friends, your routines, your environment, your work, your leisure pursuits—all the activities you engage in during your waking and sleeping hours. In other words: all that takes place around you.

Trace back what signs indicate to you that you are not making the events and details around you a priority. Simple actions, activities, behaviors, thoughts, lies, feelings, sensations, whether real or imagined, start the cascade of choices which lead to relapse or making unhealthy decisions.

> *For Henry, it was the extra water glasses on the night stand that would indicate he was not paying attention to his world. Sooner or later, other things would become cluttered and unkempt and eventually he would feel overwhelmed, hopeless, helpless, and would have to do something about it. That is when engaging in unhealthy habits, behaviors, and addictions would become an option. He would tell himself that he could pick up a drink and only have one. He forgot that lying to himself would compromise his sobriety.*

Love your Sloppy Self

Eight Tips to Help You Love YOU

1. Keep these hints on the front burner of your life. Identify your triggers and know that when there are dirty glasses on the nightstand, you are at risk.

2. Watch for the triggers that give you permission to engage in your unhealthy habits and behaviors.

3. Watch how you are feeling and pay careful attention to your fragile emotional states.

4. Watch your inner dialogue, especially self-criticism, which screams, "Caution!"

5. Watch for the tell-tale signs that compromise your health and sobriety.

6. Watch for a change in habits and routines. Go back to basics.

7. Watch how your friends and family are treating you. They often can see your lack of self-love before you can.

8. Watch your body and feel the energy as it shifts either to support your self-love, or to deny and diminish it.

What do you do when you are not being vigilant, life is getting in the way, and you are missing the clues that tell you to "Watch out!"?

Triggers can be red flags such as clues, situations, words, ideas, images, fantasies, planning, feelings, projections, visions, or excuses. Hungry, Angry, Lonely or Tired (HALT) can warn you to first *stop* and take stock of the situation...stay awake!

Think of the camping hats or mining helmets that have a spotlight attached in the front. The spotlight is always on, and you can see what is shadowed in front of you, to the side, and even behind you (by simply turning your head to look). Wear that spotlight all the time. You will be able to see in all the little corners of your life and be ready for something that might look like a trigger. A trigger is anything that could carry you over the edge into your unhealthy habits, behaviors, and addictions. If you shine the light on whatever is in your path, then it can be seen and you get to make a choice; a healthy choice.

Michael shares the secret of success is constancy of purpose.

"I recently discovered that while I make strong commitments and can be tremendously loyal and steadfast toward others, I lack the same kind of tenacity when it comes to commitments I make to myself. For example, three words: New Year's resolutions. There is no better example than my thousand decisions to swear off drinking and using drugs. After a jackpot, I promise myself never again, the price is just too great. But then, in a matter of days, sometimes less, I'm staring at the bottom of a glass or the end of a pipe.

When I make promises to other people, I'm usually much better about the follow-through. So why can't we keep promises to ourselves the way we do with others? In my case, it was the influence of alcohol and drugs. To stay true to ourselves, we must have constancy of purpose as in no other arena. Daily meetings, daily connections to others who care about us, daily prayer and attention to staying sober—in short—daily reminders that we have a habit that will kill us if we let down our guard. Without constant vigilance, we end up in jails, institutions, or worse. In the same way we keep promises to others, we must keep the promise to ourselves to stay the healthy, sober course as a primary act of Love YOU.

Love Your Slippery Self

Just Be Gentle When You Slip

Things fall. Is gravity the culprit, or is it Cupid? Trees topple, apples drop, coffee cups crash, rain comes down, and even people tumble.

Walking across a parking lot one day, I fell. There was no slippery spot, no uneven pavement, nothing heavy in my arms, and I was not in a hurry. One moment I was walking merrily along and the next I was kissing asphalt. I am sure that you have been going along, maybe even whistling a happy tune, and the next thing you know you have slipped into your bad habits and addiction.

When I slipped, I was fortunate that nothing was broken, just some badly bruised fingers and a passing feeling of embarrassment. Every time I felt the swollen black and blue of my hand, I was grateful that gravity took me down virtually unscathed.

Being your own best friend is a practice of being gentle, easy, and compassionate with yourself. Don't be too hard on yourself when you slip up, make a mistake, choose to engage in risky behavior, forget sugar is not your friend, spend more than you make, engage in Facebook drama, eat too many M&M's, or risk your sobriety by finishing the fourth glass of wine.

Pretend that falling in love with yourself is actually the gentle side of gravity, the kind that keeps your feet firmly placed beneath you; the kind that supports you and your own specialness. You are still above ground and breathing, and that's a good thing. Contemplate using the skills of loving yourself and find the self-compassion and self-forgiveness to help you start again. Loving yourself unconditionally is just the beginning of this journey. The more powerful gift is self-compassion. For compassion will trump self-esteem every time. Consider giving yourself a break when you engage in behaviors that compromise your health and well-being. You will come to understand that you really are precious and there is nothing that can ever take you down.

Make Loving Yourself a habit!

I found this piece by an anonymous author in *The Seven Habits of Highly Effective Teenagers* by Sean Covey (New York: Franklin Covey Co., 1998, p 1).

Who AM I?

I am your constant companion.
I am your greatest helper or your heaviest burden.
I will push you onward or drag you down to failure.
I am completely at your command.
Half the things you do, you might just as well turn over to me,
and I will be able to do them quickly and correctly.
I am easily managed; you must merely be firm with me.
Show me exactly how you want something done,
and after a few lessons I will do it automatically.

I am the servant of all great men.
And, alas, of all failures as well.
Those who are great, I have made great.
Those who are failures, I have made failures.
I am not a machine, though I work with all the precision of a machine.
Plus, the intelligence of a man.
You may run me for profit, or run me for ruin; it makes no difference to me.
Take me, train me, be firm with me and I will put the world at your feet.
Be easy with me, and I will destroy you.
Who am I?

I am a HABIT!

Daily Wisdom

Get your habits straight for the love of who you truly are!

Chapter 20

The Last Word on Worry

Many of us grew up with parents or families who worried all the time. Worry was a way of life, and if you didn't worry, others would think that you just "didn't care." Worry can easily become a habit and you might find yourself in the "worry straight jacket," unable to free yourself from your thoughts and your concerns.

Worry can serve as a cautionary guideline and help encourage an action that will support the best outcome for you and those you love. You can worry that the rain might come in through the windows of the porch and if you close them, you no longer have to worry about the furniture getting wet. You can worry that your ill child has a fever and if you administer the proper medication then watch for unusual changes, you can focus on spending time reading a great story to him until he falls asleep. You can worry that you might spend too much money at the mall and you can leave your credit card at home and only take a specific amount of money in order to have a relaxed and enjoyable time. You can worry that you might pick up a drink or buy some drugs and you can set your plan in place that supports your health and sobriety and enforces the love you have for your sober self.

The Dalai Lama reminds us that if you worry, worry, worry and nothing happens, you wasted your time; if you worry, worry, worry and something does happen, you wasted your time!

When there is a situation that requires your attention, you use your resources and your wisdom to solve the problem and proceed to the next encounter. To worry just zaps your energy and your creativity leaving you an emotional basket case.

Often our minds have a mind of their own and we are forever trying to comprehend and understand that incessant inner dialogue. The chatter and inner gremlins that play endless tapes of what you could have said or done, what you need to do in the future, or even how inadequate your response was to the most recent confrontation. It doesn't end there. The inner committee of brain dialogue goes on to judge your thinking and your actions. That committee of voices loves to get your emotional juices flowing and enjoys validating how wild and crazy others are in their effort to upset you. You are held hostage by the drama that ransacks your life and your judgment becomes clouded and unpredictable.

Those inner dialogues, the murmuring gremlins and conversations are not you; they are not who you truly are, and often have nothing to do with loving yourself. Those thoughts are just thoughts, and it's time for you to take responsibility for who is actually in charge; or who is "ordering lunch." Why, you are, of course!

As you learn to Love YOU, and every aspect of yourself for that matter, you will definitely consider firing that committee and begin taking charge of how you actually want to be in the world.

Being soft with yourself, compassionate with yourself, and patient with your inner wisdom will bring a silence to the ongoing chatter and an acknowledgement that you do know what to do and are more often in the right place at the right time doing the right thing.

Let's do you a favor and take the worry stone out of the backpack of life you have been carrying around. You can live with a sense of freedom when you trust that you have all the resources within you to handle just about anything that comes your way. And if there is even a hint of concern, you now know you are not alone and can always welcome help. When you are in love with yourself, you will be delighted with the results.

Love Your Softer Self

Five ways to put worry to bed

Back in 1993, Sears developed a campaign to bring female shoppers into a world of fashion apparel and personal adornments. Sears was always known as the hardware and appliance store; a man's world. Tractors, tools, and lawn mowers were image items. All of a sudden Sears was promoting jewelry and accessories as hardware for your enjoyment, and new running sneakers as shock absorbers for your athletic talents. "Come see the Softer Side of Sears" was a great success. I always liked the idea of the "softer side" of anything, and want you to think about the softer side of you.

When you are in touch with the "softer side" of yourself, your hardware is challenged and you have the option to reconsider how you live in the world.

Worry gives way to anxiety, uncertainty, and unease. Worry happens when you let your mind dwell on difficulties and problems, whether real or imagined. The original Old English word "wrygan" meant "strangle" and today's version of that word, worry, certainly strangles your very essence.

Here are four strategies that will help you put worry to bed and give yourself permission to find peace and ease in the face of adversity:

1. What your mind thinks about most of the time is what you get. This is a truth that has been around from the beginning of time. Think of worry as a negative prayer. When you pray, you are asking for your understanding of spirit to protect, offer, give, help, and guide. When you worry about something that hasn't happen yet, you are praying for that to happen. Put worry to bed and allow your positive thinking to run the show.

2. When you go to bed, decide what you will worry about and write your specific worries down on a

piece of paper or in a notebook. Keep them on the nightstand, knowing they will all be there in the morning. Now you can both enter a restful sleep.

3. Pick a special "worry time" during the day or evening. Usually an hour is more than enough. Take out your little worry notebook and just worry for that designated hour. Put your little worry book away and go on with your day until the next allotted time.

4. Find someone you trust dearly and ask them if they would be your worry partner. Ask them to worry about the problem or event that is weighing heavy in your heart. When you call them up and ask if they are worrying, they will tell you to relax and that they have it covered.

5. Remember these truths about worry.

    ♦   Worry is a negative prayer.

    ♦   Worry sets you up.

    ♦   Worry is a useless emotion.

    ♦   Worry depletes your energy.

    ♦   Worry causes anxiety.

    ♦   Worry wastes time.

And from BrainyQuotes.com, the Dalai Lama says: "When we face some problem, look at that problem and analyze if there is a way to overcome that problem. [If so,] no need to worry. Make effort. On the other hand, if the problem [has] no way to overcome, no use to worry. I believe that."

Chapter 21

Become Familiar with Your Own Brain Power

"Sorry, I just got sidetracked."

"The new video grabbed my interest, and I got sidetracked."

"What do you mean you forgot? Getting sidetracked is no excuse."

"I lost track of time. Guess I just got sidetracked."

"Before I realized it, I was thinking about something else and got sidetracked."

"Wow, my mind gets sidetracked so easily."

Have you heard these statements or even said them yourself? Getting sidetracked is a familiar process for all of us. Your sidetracked self is another aspect of your humanity that simply needs understanding, compassion, and forgiveness.

The Merriam-Webster Dictionary says that sidetracked means "to cause (someone) to talk about or do something different and less important."

The possibility of losing focus of your healthy, sober self is waiting in the wings of your theatrical life drama. There is a part of you that finds it easy to divert your attention, switch tracks, and even pay attention to events that do not support your health and well-being.

Love YOU harnesses your brainpower, and helps you build the internal muscle of choice for healthy living.

Dr. Rick Hanson is the author of *The Buddha's Brain: The Practical Neuroscience of Happiness, Love and Wisdom.* In another of his books, *Just One Thing: Developing a Buddha Brain One Simple Practice at a Time* (New Harbinger Press, 2011) he lists a number of fascinating statistics showing just how interesting and mindboggling the human brain is. Here is a summary of some of the key numbers that he reports:

♦ The brain contains one hundred billion neurons amidst another trillion support cells.

♦ The brain is just two to three percent of body weight, but consumes twenty- to twenty-five percent of the oxygen and glucose circulating in your blood.

♦ A typical neuron has connections, called synapses, with another 5000 neurons, so there are about 500 trillion synapses in the brain.

♦ Neurons fire one to fifty times a second, and sometimes faster; millions of neurons routinely form networks and fire rhythmically with each other dozens of times a second.

♦ During a single breath, a quadrillion or more neural signals travel inside your head.

♦   The number of possible combinations of 100 billion neurons firing or not—which is in principle, the quantity of potential brain states—is about ten to the millionth power. That's a one followed by a million zeros. To put this in perspective, the number of particles in the universe is estimated to be merely one followed by eighty zeros.

The recent explosion in knowledge about the brain, which has doubled in just the past twenty years, offers many practical possibilities of learning new skills and strategies that are designed to relieve distress and dysfunction, improving well-being, and deepen religious or spiritual practice.

Your mind belongs to you and only you. And the meaning of life is yours to design.

Man's Search for Meaning by Viktor Frankl (1946), made an incredible impact on my own personal life. In his acclaimed account of the concentration camps of WWII, he recognized that it is man's attitude of mind that can make all the difference.

An example of Frankl's idea of finding meaning in the midst of extreme suffering is found in his account of an experience he had while working in the harsh conditions of the Auschwitz concentration camp.

We stumbled on in the darkness, over big stones and through large puddles, along the one road leading from the camp. The accompanying guards kept shouting at us and driving us with the butts of their rifles. Anyone with very sore feet supported himself on his neighbor's arm. Hardly a word was spoken; the icy wind did not encourage talk. Hiding his mouth behind his upturned collar, the man marching next to me whispered suddenly: "If our wives could see us now! I do hope they are better off in their camps and don't know what is happening to us."

That brought thoughts of my own wife to mind. And as we stumbled on for miles, slipping on icy spots, supporting each other time and again, dragging one another up and onward, nothing was said, but we both knew: each of us was thinking of his wife. Occasionally I looked at the sky, where the stars were fading and the pink light of the morning was beginning to spread behind a dark bank of clouds. But my mind clung to my wife's image, imagining it with an uncanny acuteness. I heard her answering me, saw her smile, her frank and encouraging look. Real or not, her look was then more luminous than the sun which was beginning to rise.

A thought transfixed me: for the first time in my life I saw the truth as it is set into song by so many poets, proclaimed as the final wisdom by so many thinkers. The truth—that love is the ultimate and the highest goal to which man can aspire. Then I grasped the meaning of the greatest secret that human poetry and human thought and belief have to impart: The salvation of man is through love and in love. I under-

stood how a man who has nothing left in this world still may know bliss, be it only for a brief moment, in the contemplation of his beloved. In a position of utter desolation, when man cannot express himself in positive action, when his only achievement may consist in enduring his sufferings in the right way—an honorable way—in such a position man can, through loving contemplation of the image he carries of his beloved, achieve fulfillment. For the first time in my life I was able to understand the meaning of the words, "The angels are lost in perpetual contemplation of an infinite glory."

Why would you be interested in what happened more than half a century ago? Because choice is the word of the day. Viktor Frankl recognized that choosing an attitude of love and compassion had everything to do with survival. You have the ability to decide how you want to live a healthy and sober life, and when you begin to fall in love with yourself and stand alongside yourself with compassion, forgiveness, and empathy, you can make healthier choices.

When you are just thinking about eating those leftover cupcakes, finding the chocolate hidden in the freezer, watching another episode of your favorite series, picking up a drink, using drugs, taking an extra pain pill, working until dawn, playing endless video games, shopping in every store, adding charges to your phone with 900 calls, eating a quart of ice cream, tearing through a relationship or exploding with anger and rage, your brain has already completed the act and you are fighting a losing battle. It's too late because tunnel vision has been put into motion and it is just a matter of time before you complete the vision. Unhealthy habits, behaviors, and addictions start in your mind and in your body before you actually complete the act!

Let me say that again: Unhealthy habits, behaviors, and addictions start in your mind and in your body before you act them out. You might think you are unconscious and unaware of what is happening, but when you Love YOU and are truly your own best friend, your body sends you signals that demand your attention. Coming to know those signals and understanding their impact on your decision-making is a first step to living a healthy and sober life. Our brains are wired throughout our bodies. You have intelligence in your heart and in your gut, in your limbs and even in your face. Remember the last time you walked into a room and had a very uncomfortable gut reaction that something was just not right. Have you ever thought about doing something unhealthy and your whole body shook "No!" before you even engaged in the behaviors that would send you into an unhealthy cycle of addictive habits?

Your body knows when stressful emotions are taking over and it is time to take action. The following ideas and strategies will support your new attitude of mind that says nothing, *nothing* can sidetrack you from living a healthy and sober life.

Love Your Sidetracked Self

Sixteen Ways to Harness Your Brainpower

1. Maintain optimal hydration: Your brain is electrical and the connections run smoothly when you are hydrated. You may remember from science class that water conducts electricity. Drink a glass of water upon rising in the morning and then at least six to eight glasses throughout the day.

2. Choose a healthy diet filled with fruits, vegetables, and protein. Avoid sugars, especially foods made with High Fructose Corn Syrup (check the labels).

3. Breathe deeply first thing in the morning and just before you fall asleep. The oxygen is exactly what your brain ordered.

4. Eat a balanced breakfast which includes some protein. Your body is hungry after sleep and your brain needs the fuel to get going. Don't ever skip breakfast.

5. Get at least seven to eight hours of sleep. Going to bed before 10:00 p.m. permits you the opportunity to get the most important hours of sleep, between 10:00 p.m. and 12:00 p.m. (more about sleep in the next chapter)

6. Be still, and find a way to either meditate or sit quietly for at least ten minutes a day. Your brain

needs the down time to regroup and function at top performance.

7. Reduce the stress in your life. Find a way to reframe the "drama" so that you are not being sidetracked off into a rabbit hole with no exit. When something stressful is happening, you can ask yourself, "how will this affect me in five days, five weeks, or five years?" and this will often help to put things into perspective.

8. Practice mindfulness by paying attention to what is happening in the present moment with intention and without judgment or criticism.

9. Exercise, exercise, exercise! The latest research indicates that exercise, whether aerobic or anaerobic, will benefit your brain's health and development.

10. Find a creative hobby or activity that you will enjoy. By engaging in the creative process, you will find inner enjoyment and the process will give your brain a break.

11. We know now that our brains have a plasticity to them, which means we can actually grow new brain cells no matter how old we are. Meditation, learning a new language, a new song, a new dance, a new sport, a new craft, or a new skill offers us the opportunity to increase brain function.

12. Cultivate a loving relationship with yourself and then foster loving relationships in your world. Show up and be available to family and friends or

find a place to volunteer your time and your expertise. We are social creatures and our brains respond to the interactions and the exchanges in
community.

13. Continue to grow your gratitude list...Your mind
and your brain have the ability to send out chemicals that help you feel good. When you are grateful,
it is almost impossible to be angry or annoyed.
Gratitude is healthy for your brain; anger and resentment are extremely harmful to your health.

14. Create balance in your life. Use your brain to prior-
itize your to-do list and to make sure you are paying attention to all the areas of your life. "All work
and no play sure does make for a dull day." Consider these parts of your life: family, friends, spirit-
uality, work/profession, health, rest and relaxation, play/fun, socialization, entertainment, education, hobbies, nature...you get the idea!

15. Kiss your brain...KISS stands for Keep It Simple,
Sweetheart! Send loving energy to the masterpiece
sitting on the top of your spine; a delicate and brilliant organ encased in a protective arrangement of
bones and muscles, designed to serve you for life.
Give your brain the proper respect it deserves so
that you can Love YOU unconditionally.

16. Say to yourself often, "I wish you a glorious today
so that tomorrow will be laced with the gratitude of
yesterday."

Chapter 22

PSSST! Ever Heard About Air Time?

Giving yourself permission to live a healthy, vibrant life is a choice you make every minute of every day.

You have to *want* who you *are*
Before you can know what you *want*

Regardless of what you have heard in the past, what people have said about you and your addiction, or even how you think about yourself, you are reading this book to help yourself reframe your belief in yourself. To Love YOU means to accept all aspects of who you are just the way you are right now.

Perhaps you are disgusted and angry at your behavior and the pain you have caused yourself and others. Maybe you have been in recovery from drugs and alcohol for many years and never even considered loving yourself. It is absolutely fine that you have gotten this far in the book and are still struggling with the entire idea of self-love; but you are still reading, and that is a good thing. Repetition has a delightful way of eventually making sense and helping you create a different way of coming to know yourself.

When you accept responsibility for yourself, you are opening up the options of changing what is happening and designing what you want. When you Love YOU—all the pieces of you—you stand a better chance of loving others and making healthy choices.

Becoming your own best friend and using integrity to hold your actions to the standards of health and well-being allows you to form an interpersonal bond with yourself. Listening to your self-talk, the words you use inside your mind, sets the stage for rewiring your brain with the dialogue of sobriety.

Reaching out to others when you are in love with yourself is a new experience. There is an expression of kindness, compassion, and patience in your manner; and you then can present yourself like a dear friend. You truly can only love others when you learn to love yourself first. When Loving YOU, you have the ability to get in touch with your own feelings, your own reactions, your own sensations, your own body, and your own thoughts. That personal knowing will give you a foundation to stay connected to yourself and to others.

Find time to talk about what is happening to you. You can find an actual friend or become your own best friend. Isolation is not an option. Stay connected to others and especially to those people who can demonstrate love for you. Your unhealthy habits, behaviors, and addictions keep you in a world of disconnect. Because you are reading this book, you are about to change that. Until you can find safety in friendship, fellowship, and community, you can start a writing journal. Purchase a blank notebook that you would like to write in and divide the page down the middle. On one side of the page, write everything you are thinking; the dialogue going on in your head, no matter how ugly. On the other side, pretend you are your own best friend and dispute the dialogue with loving understanding and kindness.

Give yourself the gift of standing up for you, perhaps a standing ovation, and rise to your feet for Loving You.

Love Your Standing O Self

Seven ways to applaud YOU

1. Pretend that you are on stage all day long and no matter what you do, you will receive applause from everyone watching.

2. Download applause sound effects from YouTube and listen to it a couple of times every day.

3. Look in the mirror and smile; take a couple of bows for your tremendous effort to be happy.

4. Find a blue-ribbon award and hang it in your office, by your desk, or even in the kitchen. When someone asks about the blue ribbon, simply say you won first prize (and know that it's for loving yourself).

5. Buy an old trophy at a tag sale and keep it near your bed or on your desk. You know that you are a winner in life.

6. Practice random acts of kindness, and don't tell anyone

7. Say "thank you" more often...and mean it!

Susan's sister was asked to present her with the ten-year coin at an AA meeting. When you are clean and sober over time, everyone celebrates *you!*

Here is the speech that was shared at Susan's celebration:

> *On August 13, 2001, Susan made the decision to stop the cycle of addiction, of self-medicating; she stopped hiding her pain behind the use of alcohol and drugs. Susan made a conscious decision to take control of her life. On this day, she began to release the negative habits that had grown so familiar and also the lifestyle that had given her the false idea of safety addiction provides.*
>
> *With an ever-increasing sense of self-acceptance, self-worth, and most importantly, forgiveness for herself and others, Susan stands here today with ten years of hard-earned sobriety and gratitude. With the help of AA and her sponsors, she tackled the deep, painful, and honest work that is necessary to break the cycle of self-destruction. Susan has changed the path of her life. She took the power away from the painful experiences of the past and put that power toward living a life of compassion toward herself and toward others.*

Today, Susan's life is heathy and happy, but not perfect, as perfection is not her goal. She knows that striving for perfection in the past, present, or future is neither realistic nor possible.

I read a quote somewhere a while ago and wrote it down because of the powerful message regarding forgiveness of the self and of others. The quote reads:

"Forgiveness means giving up all hope for a better past."

I am honored to give Susan her ten-year coin. As a family we celebrate her success. Also I feel that somehow even though their time on this earth has passed, our father and mother are also feeling joy and gratitude today, content in knowing that by sharing her story and strength of character, Susan is able to help others.

Chapter 23

Sleep, Health, Sobriety, and Your Brain

The latest brain research supports the concept that sleep is essential for good health, brain function, well-being, and living a productive life. At this point in your life, it could be that you are considering the possibility of making healthy habits, supportive behaviors, and sobriety a lifelong permanent partner. You want more than anything to stay healthy and sober in order to enjoy the rest of your days here on Earth.

If your inner gremlins and unhealthy habits, behaviors, and addictions have made your life unmanageable up to this point, Love YOU will carry you through the maze of making wise choices and wholesome decisions. Remember:

Healthy choices = fewer problems.

The fast pace of today's world continues to set you up for the challenges of staying vigilant to self-care and self-love. Taking time to rest, renew, restore, refresh, and revitalize yourself demands a fail-safe plan of action. To say you are tired and "should" take a nap is ridiculous if you don't actually do it. Take that nap and then start getting to sleep earlier.

If you are at all tired during the day, sleepy after lunch, fatigued when you get home, yawning before you get to work, suffering from brain fog, or are forgetful or unfocused, it is possible that you just might not be getting enough sleep.

While you are learning to Love YOU, start by waking up to your precious self and realizing all the positive things you deserve in life and that you are on your way to making good decisions. Those decisions lead to choices for a different behavior and you leave behind your unhealthy habits of eating sugar, smoking, wine, beer, drugs, gambling, food, sex, work, candy, porn, prescriptions pills, or shopping.

Your body is the vehicle that carries you around in life. The warrantee is null and void if you neglect your health and choose to put yourself at risk. The human body is designed to function at top performance with good nutrition, appropriate rest, adequate fresh air, regular movement and exercise, and plenty of water. If you make choices to ignore the requirements of a healthy body, you are just an accident waiting to happen.

If you have not been as healthy as you would like, if your bad habits are still lingering in your life, and if your addictions have compromised your sobriety, then you have been in an ongoing accident, and it is time to get yourself up and humming again. Only you can make that decision, and when you Love YOU enough, you will begin to know what to do.

Love your Slumbering Self

Twenty Ways to Get a Good Night's Sleep

1. Make sleep a priority and plan your slumber accordingly.

2. Go to bed earlier and wake up earlier. The sleep between 10:00 p.m. and 12:00 a.m. is the most restorative for your brain.

3. Start getting ready for bed with a routine. Personal hygiene, meditation, prayer, reading, and relaxing. Avoid stressful and stimulating television. Find something funny to watch on TV. Humor helps the mind release and calm down.

4. Wear comfortable clothing, choose the right pillow, and have enough covers. Keep your feet warm and toasty.

5. Try to eat you last meal or even a snack at least four hours before going to sleep. Digestion functions better when you are upright.

6. You can eat something light, maybe an English muffin with peanut butter, yogurt, or warm milk and graham crackers right before bed.

7. Keep the room dark and quiet. If you are used to the TV going all night, begin to change that habit.

Darkness is essential for your brain to re-charge. You can use white noise like the ocean or a forest breeze (or just a fan) and you can also use an eye mask.

8.   Put your worries on the nightstand. Write a list of things on your mind so you do not have to mull them over while trying to sleep.

9.   Do some stretching or yoga to relax your muscles and your spirit.

10. Climb into bed with the intention of having a good night's sleep because you deserve it. Tell yourself you can do whatever needs to be done in the morning.

11. Settle into the bed, snuggle down, arrange the covers so they are comfortable, and begin to relax your body.

12. Use a meditation, guided visualization, or a body scan to release the tension from your muscles and calm your mind. Free on www.mindfulrp.com, the website for Mindfulness Based Relapse Prevention.

13. Begin to breathe slowly and evenly. Counting the in-breaths and the out-breaths until you get to ten. If you find that your mind is wandering and you are thinking of something other than your breath, start over at one.

14. If you are still thinking too much, find something mindless to practice, like your times tables.

15. Feel yourself drifting off to sleep and know that your nighttime journey is waiting for you.

16. If you wake in the night to go to the bathroom, keep the lights low and your eyes mostly closed so you can get right back to the business of sleeping.

17. You are planning seven to eight of uninterrupted sleep. Eight and a half is the average for most adults.

18. Keep the clock at a distance or turned away so you are not looking at it throughout the night. Use a soft alarm if you need one.

19. Keep a journal by the bed to record any dreams you might remember upon walking.

20. Place a glass of water by the bed and drink it upon waking. Your body is dehydrated in the morning and water will start your juices flowing and your energy moving.

The following excerpt is from an article I wrote to help you wake up with a blink, a wink, and a smile! Enjoy!

When you first awaken and are just coming into consciousness, you have a powerful opportunity to begin your day in a positive way. Those few seconds—from sleep to awareness—matter most. Those first moments when you realize you are no longer sleeping can make a positive impact on your reality for the entire day.

Find a mirror and take a look at yourself. Now, blink your eyes and really take a good look at yourself. Blink them again, and then wink at yourself. If you can't wink, just pretend that you can. Smile! Even if you feel a little silly...do it again...blink, wink, and smile.

Think about how you awaken in the morning.

Does the alarm jar you from a delicious dream? Does the sun tickle your face? Do your eyes open on their own? Do you smell the coffee brewing? Does someone call your name? Does your bed partner snuggle closer to you? Do you hear the cat purr, or does the dog lick the sleep from your eyes?

It does not matter...you are awake, and that is the moment to set a positive and productive day in motion. So, seize that moment!

Research shows that thoughts and feelings of gratitude and appreciation have a significant impact on the chemistry of your brain. Your first thought of the day is your key to what comes next. When that thought is of gratitude and appreciation, your motivation, desire, intention, creativity, and energy will create your impending success.

Your first thought, image, vision, impression, or feeling needs to be one of gratitude. Think of something that warms your heart. It can be something big or small, but whatever it is, it should give you a warm feeling around your heart. That heartwarming will change the chemistry in both your brain and your body. Here are some examples of heartwarming thoughts:

I am so grateful for my breath this morning.

I am so grateful for the warmth and the comfort of my bed.

I am so grateful for the fact that all my parts are moving.

I am so grateful I am free of the headache I had last night.

I am so grateful for the love I feel for my family, kids, my partner....

I am so grateful morning is here.

I am so grateful for the rain against the windowpane today....

Feel the presence of the moment. Sense your eyelashes touching each other. Notice the soft breeze they make when they open and close. Get ready to smile. Smile, even though there is no mirror... Next...WINK...Wink at yourself, at the morning, at the moment, at the possibilities. Enjoy yourself, and sit up to roll out of bed and begin your glorious, delightful, energetic, positive, productive, and fun-filled day!

Chapter 24

How to Make Breathing Work for You

It is time to talk about the breath—your breath. Think of your breath as the life force that makes it possible for you to be alive. The breath is the only thing that you can count on 24/7. Imagine your breath as a very dear friend, someone who will show up for you no matter what. You breathe and you live.... it is that simple.

When someone dies, they expire on the out breath. Your desire to stay alive keeps you breathing in and out, over and over again. The breath is your life force and for many of us, we forget that the breath is even there. The physical biology of the human body is a miracle. The breath keeps coming and sometimes it feels as if the breath is actually breathing *you*. When was the last time you stopped and thought about your breath?

Do it now. Read the next few lines and follow along with the instructions:

Take a breath in and see if you can follow what happens. Notice the air that comes in at the end of your nose, notice the rise and fall of your chest, notice the sound, pay attention to how long it takes to breathe in and then exhale.

Pay attention to the temperature of the air, it is cool coming in and warm going out?

The average adult will breathe twelve to twenty times in a minute. There are a variety of factors that can influence the number of breaths you take. Physical problems, stress, lung damage, exercise, and activity can have an impact on your capacity to breathe easily and effortlessly.

You can count your breaths while you are at rest and you might be able to slow the pace down to six or ten breaths a minute. When you can slow your breathing down, you will change how you are feeling. Your attention becomes focused on the air coming in at the end of your nose and awareness becomes aligned with the pace at which you are operating. By slowing down, you have a chance to stop what is happening around you and give yourself an opportunity to make a healthy choice of behavior.

When you stop and slow down, life becomes more manageable and you even see clearer, sense better, and hear more information. There is an energy about rushing and becoming frantic that causes your thinking brain to short circuit. Consider the practice of slowing down and breathing consciously. Conscious breathing means to pay attention to the air that comes into your body and then be aware of the air that leaves your body. You will be initiating a practice of mindfulness, paying attention, in the present moment, on purpose and without judgment...to your breath.

When you give yourself permission to slow down, you will be able to witness the delicate internal wisdom that bubbles up to the surface.

The part that is Loving YOU will know exactly what you are doing when you slow down and that part of you will come to your aid like a warrior, ready to protect you from your own worst decisions.

At the beginning of *Love YOU*, you learned an acronym for the word SOBER or "Sacrificing Obnoxious Behaviors Encourages Respect."

The purpose of the SOBER acronym is to set the stage for tackling not only the inner cranky gremlins of your thinking but the habits, behaviors, and addictions that seem to run our lives.

Throughout the book, we have been looking at habits, behaviors, and addictions through a different lens, with intentions of changing the choices we make for our ongoing well-being.

The SOBER Breathing Space is a skill taught in the course "Mindfulness Based Relapse Prevention." The course is based on the mindfulness work of Jon Kabat Zinn and the work of relapse prevention by Alan Marlatt, Sarah Bowen, and Neha Chawla. I have included the skill of SOBER Breathing as a way to begin practicing a new skill of loving yourself.

From Mindfulness-Based Relapse Prevention (MBRP), www.mindfulrp.com, Bowen, Chawla, and Marlatt (2010) is a novel treatment approach developed at the Addictive Behaviors Research Center at the University of Washington, for individuals in recovery for addictive behaviors.

> *The program is designed to bring practices of mindful awareness to individuals suffering from the addictive trappings of the mind. MBRP practices are intended to foster increased awareness of triggers, destructive habitual patterns, and automatic reactions that seem to control many of our lives. The mindfulness practices in MBRP are designed to help us pause and observe the present moment. We learn to respond in ways that serves us, rather than react in ways that are detrimental to our health and happiness. Ultimately, we are working towards freedom from deeply ingrained and often catastrophic habits.*

Love Your SOBER Self

Skills to Help Orchestrate Healthy Decisions

From the Mindfulness Based Relapse Prevention course, we know that staying sober is always a choice. Having skills and strategies to help you make wise and healthy decisions will support your success.

SOBER Breathing Space Skill

You can do this exercise almost anywhere, anytime because it is very brief and quite simple. This is an especially useful exercise when we find ourselves in a stressful or high risk situation. Often when we are triggered by things in ourselves or in our environment, we tend to go into automatic pilot, which can result in our behaving in ways that are not in our best interest. This is a technique based on the SOBER acronym that can be used to help us step out of that automatic mode and become more aware and mindful or our actions.

S...Stop

O...Observe

B...Breathe

E...Expand

R...Respond

S = STOP

The first step is to stop and slow down right where you are, and make the choice to step out of the automatic pilot by bringing awareness to this moment.

O = OBSERVE

Now just observe what is happening in this moment in your body, your emotions, and your thoughts.

B = BREATHE

Gather your attention and focus simply on the sensations of breathing.

E = EXPAND

Expand awareness again to include a sense of the whole body and the situation you are presently in.

R = RESPOND

Now notice that you can respond with awareness and can make the choice on how you want to be in the world from a place of awareness, strength, and clarity.

The SOBER Breathing Space Skill works best after you spend time practicing with easier and ordinary situations. Rather than being irritated about someone cutting in line: Stop yourself, observe your body, breathe for a moment, expand your body awareness, and respond from a calmer and kinder point of view. Ask yourself, "What difference does one person make, in the larger scheme of things?" You'll feel better about yourself when you choose not to re-act out of anger and frustration.

How about when your child or a friend tells you something unsettling? Use the SOBER skill to hear the explanation and decide not to overreact. When you are calm and approachable, they will be encouraged to trust you again.

When someone cuts you off in traffic, rather than engage in road rage, practice the SOBER skill to keep your own blood pressure down. Becoming angry does nothing more than cause *you* problems, not the other person.

When you are at risk of engaging in an addictive behavior, STOP...before you are seduced by that automatic pilot.

Stop before you take another bite of chocolate

Stop before you go out the door for a scratch ticket

Stop before you open Facebook

Stop before you park in front of the bar

Stop before you turn on the TV

Stop before you walk into the mall

Stop before you reach for the pills

Stop before you turn on the computer

Stop before you make another appointment

Stop before you throw something

...And so on.

The more you practice the complete skill, the easier it will be for you to first stop! We always want to move things too quickly. Often the automatic pilot is running the show and we are left trying to clean up a mess we did not want to happen. Learn to stop and be present and be patient, before you react, respond and regret what you might say or do.

Chapter 25

Four Simple Choices for a Healthy Life

When you are not in love with yourself, when you are not loving all the parts of you, especially your very precious self, you are between a rock and a hard place. Dilemma means there are two choices that you are not sure about; the choice of being healthy or sober and the choice of falling in love with yourself. What if you thought of that life challenge as the Love YOU dilemma? Can you choose both at the same time, and could you start with Loving YOU?

At first glance, neither choice is desirable because the dilemma would mean that the real decision would command you to change.

The truth is though, that everything changes. Life is in perpetual motion and change is what keeps us going. You might want to consider that change is your ticket for transformation, and transformation is the ride towards unconditional love. The self-love you are cultivating is a journey and an ongoing process, your process, which is a good thing. The following quotes ring a sober sound:

The key to change...is to let go of fear ~Rosanne Cash

Nobody makes a greater mistake than he who did nothing because he could do only little.
~Edmund Burke

Nobody can go back and start a new beginning, but anyone can start today and make a new ending.
~Maria Robinson

For everything you have missed, you have gained something else, and for everything you gain you lose something else. ~Ralph Waldo Emerson

The doors we open and close each day decide the lives we live. ~Flora Whittemore

Sometimes it's the smallest decisions that can change your life forever. ~Keri Russell

What you leave behind is not what is engraved in stone monuments, but what is woven into the lives of others. ~Pericles

There is nothing wrong with change, if it is in the right direction. ~Winston Churchill

If you give up the bad habits and addictive behaviors, then you are losing perhaps your very best friend. What would you do instead? How would you be in the world? Where would you go if you were Hungry, Angry, Lonely, or Tired (HALT)? Who would be with you when you were sad? How would you deal with the urges or the cravings? When would you ever trust yourself to do the right thing? Your addiction has taken you far from the joys of living a flourishing life, but perhaps, has kept you focused on freedom from pain and heartache.

Rather than being in such a dilemma, just decide to love yourself first. The thought of telling yourself that your self-love is a priority will take a commitment and a soul declaration of trust...relax into that trust and say simply:

"I love me and there is nothing I can do about it!"

You are learning to become your own best friend, and moving past the friendship you had developed with your unhealthy habits and addictions. The addictive behaviors were never meant to be in your best interest, but to keep you from truly loving your very own precious self. When you come to know and love yourself, from an authentic and genuine place, you will adapt the attitude of a loyal and confident friend, one who will show up for you over and over again.

Love Your Simple Self

Four Simple Choices for a Sober Life

1. Love yourself

2. Eat well

3. Exercise regularly

4. Rest more often

Chapter 26
What About Reinforcing Self-Compassion?

According to the internet dictionaries, sympathy is characterized and preceded by compassion. Being sympathetic means to have a special affinity or mutual relationship with another where congeniality and connection are in harmony.

Coming to know your sympathetic self gives you the opportunity to offer compassion and empathy to your very precious essence. Let's take a look at the various meanings for sympathetic and apply them to our interest in loving every part of ourselves.

Neurology and neuroscience identify the sympathetic nervous system as the active branch of our anatomy that initiates the fight, flight, freeze, or faint response. It doesn't matter if the threat is actual or just perceived, our response is usually automatic. If we are not careful, and don't stay aware of our intentions, the response can become automatic. The nervous system energizes the body and we are able to flee a predator, fight a foe, complete a project, and find the stamina to "keep going."

The stress response can come in many forms and often it is the trigger that can send us searching for our unhealthy habits and behaviors or our drug of choice.

- ◆ A critical comment from a co-worker, and we are eating more chocolate

- ◆ An extra bit of change, and we are buying a lottery ticket

- ◆ An unexpected phone call, and we are headed for a drink

- ◆ A feeling of loneliness, and we are on the Internet

- ◆ An upsetting argument, and we are looking for a reason to explode

If you are not loving yourself and holding your health and sobriety as top priorities, then the automatic pilot of stress around loneliness, hurt, sadness, rejection, and incompetence takes over.

Sometimes thinking outside the box can give us a new perspective when working to understand a different idea. Let's use some of the definitions for "sympathetic" in order to clarify the significance of Loving YOU.

Music theory recognizes strings that resonate without contact as having a sympathetic ability. Perhaps we can adapt that same theory and believe that the "strings of our hearts" resonate with the inner desire to be loved. We can't really touch those strings, but we know that they vibrate with love and care for ourselves.

In religion, magic, and anthropology, like affects like is an intelligent way to validate your own self. You like yourself and sooner or later you will influence your ability to truly be in love with all the aspects of yourself.

Similar to sympathetic detonation (when one bomb explodes it sets off the one next to it), if the love you have for others is strong and you practice loving others unconditionally, then it is inevitable that the love you have for others will ignite a flame for your own inner being.

Sympathetic resonant is held in your very cells from the beginning of your existence. You were pure love when you arrived as an infant. The external vibration of love is consistent and powerful and your precious self is responding to that energy. You need only surrender, relax, and allow yourself to be held in the embrace of existing love.

And finally, in psychology, sympathy is a feeling of compassionate identification with another. When you Love YOU, you are offering compassion to yourself; that "other" is you! We buy sympathy cards for people who have had a loved one pass away. Sending a sympathy card is social protocol for telling someone we care about how they are feeling. The following is a collection of words from sympathy cards I have received in the past. The messages can be applied to your journey of accepting the part of you that loves you unconditionally and with a sympathetic heart.

Please remember you're not on this road alone. Others will be beside you in thought and prayer until you reach a place of healing and peace.

It is not how long the flower blooms, but how beautiful.

May words of comfort rest gently upon your heart and in time may they become words of healing.

The watching and the wanting...the hanging on and the letting go...It's been a long and difficult journey and now a new one begins.

Sea shells remind us that every passing life leaves something beautiful behind. With heartfelt sympathy, praying for your peace.

With sympathy in the loss of your good and faithful friend.

There is a fine line between pity and sympathy. When you reflect on being pitted, you would rather someone have sympathy for you than pity. Pity brings with it a sense of judgment, regret, disappointment, and sorrow.

I don't want you to pity me. I would rather have you love me with compassion and hope.

Hope. It is the only thing stronger than fear.
~ The Hunger Games, the movie

Now sometimes, when things are going so poorly, you just might feel like having that pity party for yourself. Might be a good idea as long as it has the intention of giving you a chance to take a breather, regroup without judgment, make a plan to integrate the events, and recommit yourself to healthy choices so there will be a future with fewer problems. Limit the party to one hour or less and conclude with an intention to reignite the firm sense of self-love and cherishing attitude towards yourself.

Some of us can very easily say to ourselves:

"I like who I am." "I'm really good at...." "I am a good person." "I really am OK." "People like me." "I have people I truly love in my life." "I feel blessed." "I know I have made mistakes." "I forgive myself."

But when it comes to actually loving yourself, that's when we seem to run into difficulty. And people stop at the word "love." But why? Is it that loving yourself demands an unconditional acceptance of who you are? Who you are is exactly who you were meant to be. The struggle to love all aspects of yourself is an ongoing adventure and challenges every cell in the fabric of your essence to declare that self-love is real and powerful.

You have a purpose and a reason for living. Your healthy, sober self is waiting and wanting to relish the opportunity to find peace, happiness, and joy in who you are, right now. Not tomorrow; not when you stop drinking; not when you lose weight; not when you no longer owe money; not when you choose a stable relationship; not when you find intimacy in friendship and partnership; not if you avoid the race track; not if you turn off the TV; not when you quit your job; not when you stop hurting or exploding...but *right now*, just as you are.

From the movie *Hugo*, the little boy who fixes clocks and tinker toys tells his new friend,

> *...I'd imagine the whole world was one big machine.*
> *Machines never come with extra parts, you know.*
> *They always come with the exact amount they need.*
> *So I figured if the entire world was one big machine,*
> *I couldn't be an extra part, I had to be here for some*
> *reason and that means you have to be here for some*
> *reason, too.*

You are here for a reason, and learning to love your sympathetic self will reinforce the self-compassion so vital to your health and well-being.

No need to be afraid anymore, for the love you are cultivating for yourself will lighten the fear load in your heart and in your life.

Love Your Sympathetic Self

Nine Ways to Reinforce Self-Compassion

Here are ten ways for you to use to reinforce your ability for self-compassion:

1. Monitor your inner self-talk and keep the words you say to yourself positive, soft, and loving.

2. Apologize to yourself for making judgments that are hurtful to you and others.

3. Be patient and loving to yourself when you are rushed and frantic.

4. Buy yourself flowers on a regular basis and stop often to enjoy them.

5. Offer appreciation and gratitude to yourself for making it through each and every day.

6. Be quiet and sit still for a short while each day. Imagine you are helping someone to experience sadness and loss and are offering tenderness and care. If sadness shows up, offer a tissue or a hanky to yourself so that the tears can flow gracefully as you love your sympathetic self.

7. When there is a call of sympathy for yourself, there is a sense of compassion and tenderness towards who you are in the world. Offering forgiveness to yourself is a powerful way to release the energy from the past.

8. Practice the "Loving Kindness Meditation," saying to yourself: "May I be safe and well protected. May I be happy. May I be healthy. May I be peaceful and may I live with ease."

9. Act as if you are your own best friend and rely on you for the same kind, compassionate, caring advice you would give to your actual best friend.

Chapter 27

Love Your Stunning, Strobe Light, Spiritual Self

If you have gotten this far, then it is time for you come to understand you are basically a perfect spiritual being, having a perfect spiritual experience, in a human body. Life is not complicated. It just is, and you are simply perfect, just the way you are. Why not entertain that thought; the alternative is rather discouraging. Most of your life you have spent beating yourself up, being hard on yourself, kicking yourself while you were down, giving up on yourself, and even abandoning yourself.

What would happen if you began to believe and trust in the light that shines within you as your right to be human and to flourish in life? That belief might not happen over-night, but your willingness to consider sobriety and your ability to make healthy choices begins with a decision to love yourself first, unconditionally.

Your quality of brightness reflects the shine that is there naturally, like the sun; her presence graces our plan-et Earth with energy, light and life force. The light within you has been there since day one—your birth, and only you can claim its spectacular, stunning strobe light essence.

The transformation into Loving YOU takes courage, patience, persistence, practice, willingness, faith, perseverance, kindness, friendship, gentleness, and warm, loving care. A tall order of personal qualities—are you up for the challenge?

Seven Ways to Shine Your Inner Light

1. Imagine that you have an inner flame glowing just behind your heart. Your body is yours to transform in any way you want. Give yourself permission to design and create whatever you need to fall in love with yourself.

2. When you want to feel more love for yourself, turn the flame up higher and let it radiate throughout your body, mind, and spirit.

3. A strobe light reflects the light from objects it shines on, especially the white one. Act as if your light magnifies the light from others and together you make the world a brighter place. Put others in the spotlight and see how they smile!

4. Spend some time each day just sitting still; ten or fifteen minutes is all it will take on a daily basis. Find a comfortable upright position, on a cushion, a chair, or a couch and just sit still. You can focus on your breathing or a simple mantra, such as "peace," "love," "joy," and so on.

5. Your inner light glows from within. You can express your radiance through your smile, your eyes,

and even your posture. When you Love YOU, the warmth in your expressions, the tenderness on your face, the compassion in your voice, and kindness in your gestures, validate a genuine commitment to live a life of love, health, and well-being.

6. When you are spectacular, you are beautiful, eye-catching, and in the spotlight of loving who you are. Not an arrogant stance, but a sincere and genuine love of self. When someone asks, "how are you doing today," tell them, "I am simply spectacular, thanks for asking!"

7. Find a way to put yourself on a spiritual journey. Find a path that will resonate with your light, your self-love, your lifestyle, and your passion. Do it soon and do it often.

It is the light within you that shines through as you make healthy choices to live a beautiful life.

Chapter 28

Love Your Sunshine Self

The earth rotates around the sun. It is the sun that offers planet earth the opportunity to exist. The sun has been around for more than 4.5 billion years and can hold 1.3 million earths inside its sphere. How tiny we are in comparison. The energy given by the sun contains everything needed to sustain life on this big blue marble we call home.

You might ask, what does the sun have to do with my effort to *love myself?* It seems a little unusual, but recognizing the power of our sun can reinforce your understanding of your own inner light. The sun warms the planet, sustains life, and makes it possible for us to see. As you build your muscle of loving yourself, all aspects of yourself, you will come to know your own power. You will feel your own warmth, witness your own ability to sustain your healthy life, and as if by magic, be able to see more clearly when making healthy decisions.

The sun radiates its light everywhere. As you learn to love your sunshine self, you too will radiate your light, everywhere. Love YOU and practice the skills and ideas in this little collection; you will give yourself the opportunity to heal, be healthy, and be hopeful for an awesome thriving life and a successful future laced with joy. One of my favorite jazz pieces is "On the Sunny Side of the Street" by Diana Krall. When you look for "Sun" in the title of songs, it's a trip down memory lane with melodies and lyrics that stick to your soul. Here are some that offer inspiration...enjoy!

"Here Comes the Sun" ~The Beatles

"Good Day Sunshine" ~The Beatles

"I'll Follow the Sun" ~The Beatles

"Don't let the Sun Catch You Crying" ~George Michael and Elton John

"Everyday Sunshine" ~Fishbone

"California Sun" ~The Rivieras

"Aquarius Let the Sunshine In" ~The 5th Dimension

"House of the Rising Sun" ~The Animals

"It's a Sunshine Day" ~The Brady Bunch

"A Place in the Sun" ~Stevie Wonder

"Soak Up the Sun" ~Sheryl Crow

"Sun is Shining" ~Bob Marley

"Sunny Afternoon" ~The Kinks

"Sunrise" ~Norah Jones

"Sunshine on My Shoulder" ~John Denver

"Tequila Sunrise" ~Eagles

"Warmth of the Sun" ~The Beach Boys

"We'll Sing in the Sunshine" ~Gale Garnett

"You are My Sunshine" ~Jimmie Davis

"You Are the Sunshine of My Life" ~Stevie Wonder

Chapter 29

Love Your Signature Self

Sign your name with pride and delight in who you are! Your signature is more powerful than you think. Based on the science of graphology, your handwriting comes directly from your brain. When your muscles are moving freely, the electrical currents from your brain are orchestrating the activity. In a state of familiar relaxed writing, your shoulder, arm, and hand are moving the writing instrument freely. The thoughts are flowing from your mind and your ego is somewhere at rest.

The central nervous system controls the movements that are related to your internal state of mind, physically, psychologically, emotionally, and spiritually. Handwriting analysis has been around for hundreds of years and has been used to discover and reveal the character and the essence of the person doing the writing.

What does your signature represent about you? Since you are reinventing yourself by falling in love with all that is you, why not take a serious look at how you write and consider the information coming from your own beautiful brain.

There are free assessments and information available on the Internet. Google "handwriting or your signature" and have some fun!

Chapter 30

Love Your Sweet Self

You Have Come This Far…Just Do It:
Love YOU!

Here we are, almost at the end of this little book, or are we at the beginning of a new way of life to Love YOU? Each of the chapters has been designed to focus on an adjective that begins with the letter "S." Maybe it is my attempt at helping your beautiful human mind to remember how precious you are and that nothing happens until you learn to love yourself—all the aspects of yourself.

The human pallet has four major tastes: sour, bitter, salty, and sweet. All of those tastes could hold their own addictive cycle, but for these purposes, lets us use "sweet" to mean something other than the food we taste. When you are Loving YOU, you have a pleasant taste of character; untainted, pure and fresh; a gratifying sense of living the sweet life.

I did say in the very beginning of this book, that repetition and practice are vital to helping you learn how to Love YOU. We were taught growing up that "practice makes perfect," but the truth is, "practice makes permanent." When you practice unhealthy decisions, your life becomes unmanageable and those decisions become a permanent way of living.

Here is your chance to practice something different, so that love for yourself becomes a permanent practice. Remember that it takes "perfect practice to make a skill permanent." Cultivate and develop the skills that help you Love YOU and make it a permanent quality of your life. By reviewing the chapters and identifying one of the important and memorable components, you just might be willing to consider that when you Love YOU, that thought becomes an option you can and will entertain.

- ♦ Love Your Significant Self. Know you are important!

- ♦ Love Your Smart Self. Know you are brilliant!

- ♦ Love Your Steadfast Self. Know your triggers.

- ♦ Love Your Scared Self. Know that hope is stronger than fear.

- ♦ Love Your Sabotaging Self. Know your plan and know it cold.

- ♦ Love Your Smiling Self. Know there is no stress when you smile.

- ♦ Love Your Sleepy Self. Know you can always do it.

- ♦ Love Your Sensitive Self. Know how to be graceful.

- ♦ Love Your Solid Self. Know your body.

- Love Your Shameful Self. Know compassion and forgiveness.

- Love Your Sincere Self. Know and trust your inner wisdom.

- Love Your Stubborn Self. Know your strong-willed self.

- Love Your Solo Self. Know you are precious!

- Love Your Shining Self. Know there is a glow within.

- Love Your Star Dust Self. Know and trust you are pure love.

- Love Your Sprinting Self. Know how to stay the course.

- Love Your Slippery Self. Know how to be gentle with yourself.

- Love Your Softer Self. Know how to live worry-free.

- Love Your Sidetracked Self. Know your brain potential.

- Love Your Standing O Self. Know how to be your own best cheerleader.

- Love Your Slumbering Self. Know the importance of sleep.

- Love Your SOBER Self. Know how to breathe.

- Love Your Simple Self. Know how to make it easy.

- Love Your Sympathetic Self. Know self-care

- Love Your Spectacular Self. Know your spirit

- Love Your Sunshine Self. Know your energy connection

- Love Your Signature Self. Know how to be proud of you

- Love Your Sweet Self. Know how to fall in love with you

Chapter 31

The ABCs of Love YOU!

I am._____ (fill in the blank with one from the list).

Use the following list to remind yourself that you are precious, special, and capable of living a healthy and sober life.

Write each word on a 3 x 5 card and keep the stack available to review throughout the day. Flip the deck while at a stop light, while on the phone, during TV commercials—you get the idea. Read each word before you go to sleep at night and again when you wake up in the morning. You can also add your own words as you begin to believe in all that you are becoming.

Choose one of the descriptive adjectives to focus on for one entire day and use it as a mantra all day long. Example: I am accepting, I am brave, I am curious, I am delightful, I am funny, I am light-hearted....

Here's an example of the ABCs of Love YOU:

A...Accepting

B...Brave

C...Curious

D...Delightful

E...Engaging

F...Fearless

G...Gracious, grateful

H...Happy

I...Ingenious, individual

J...Joyous

K...Knowledgeable

L...Lively

M...Magnificent

N...Noble

O...Original

P...Patient

Q...Quiet

R...Robust

S...Steady, silly, superb, strong

T...Tenacious tender

U...Understanding

V...Vital, virile, vibrant

W...Wonderful, wearing the world as a loose garment

X...Xanadu

Y...Yearning

Z...Zealous

Chapter 32

Did You S.T.U.B. Your Toe?

A children's story to encourage delight in learning how to develop the skills to be able to quiet the gremlins, tame the unhealthy habits, behaviors, and addictions in your life, and make thoughtful decisions and healthy choices.

Selah was in a hurry...a big hurry. It had been a terrible day at school, and all she wanted to do was get home and play with her new fairy dolls that she had gotten for her birthday.

She could already imagine the tea party with her dolls. They would drink warm tea and eat the pink cupcakes that she had hidden in the cupboard. There was no time for stepping on cracks in the sidewalk, or twirling in the daisies along the path home.

When she opened the front door, she dropped her backpack in the mudroom. Selah has always loved to kick off her shoes, peel off her socks, and wiggle her toes all around. Somehow, being barefoot had always helped Selah to leave the day's worries behind and focus on the excitement of the present moment. After all, nothing else really mattered.

Selah ran down the hall faster than any fairy wings could take her. Charging into the kitchen without watching where she was going changed the entire afternoon for Selah.

"Ouch!" she screamed, as she jammed her pinky toe into the heavy kitchen chair that had been left near the counter.

It hurt so much that she saw stars on the ceiling and tears began streaming down her cheeks. Mom wasn't home, so she began to panic. Selah could feel a frightening energy traveling through her entire body. As the pain and fear mounted, she began to believe that she had broken that little pinky toe. There was no way she could stop the pain, so she did the only thing she could do—she began to cry even harder!

She grabbed her foot and lay on the floor yelling and squirming. All of a sudden, as if by magic, she heard a playful and musical voice coming from somewhere above her. Little did she know that this voice would change her entire day yet again.

"Selah, did you stub your toe?"

Selah stood up, and through tear-filled eyes, began to look all around the room for the source of the voice.

"Did you stub your toe?" Selah heard again.

When Selah turned towards the kitchen counter, she could not believe her eyes. On the counter, in front of the toaster, was a tiny little pixie all dressed in soft lemon yellow satin.

"Hi, Selah! Welcome home from school," said the little pixie.

Selah was so surprised, she forgot about her toe hurting. She whispered, "Who are you?"

"Why, I'm your Heart Wisdom Pixie from the fifth dimension, and I live in a pocket right here," said the pixie as she flew over and placed her soft little hand over Selah's heart.

"I am always with you," said the little pixie. "My responsibility is to help you make healthy and thoughtful decisions. You may not know this yet, but you already have the power to make great decisions."

"Do you have a name?" asked Selah.

"Morning Glory, or MG for short, because I love breakfast better than any other meal. Breakfast welcomes each new day. You stubbed your toe, didn't you, Selah?" the pixie said.

"I sure did. It really, really hurt," whimpered Selah as she remembered the pain.

"When you stubbed your toe, everything stopped, right? You even stopped thinking about the tea party you were planning," MG declared.

"I guess you're right," acknowledged Selah.

"Then, when you realized what happened, you began to worry about your poor toe," said MG.

"Yep," Selah said. "I was afraid that I broke my little baby toe."

"So now you see that your toe did not break. You just really hurt it. Your body knew something happened and the signal of pain went right to your brain. Your toe got hot and you started to cry," Morning Glory said softly.

"When you stop to take a deep breath, and then another deep breath, you will realize, that even though your toe hurts, you don't need to panic," said MG.

"Yeah," said Selah, "I can remember that it's not the end of the world and I'll be fine. Maybe if I just keep thinking about the tea party, I won't be so scared and the pain won't be nearly as bad."

"That's exactly it, Selah. You are learning so fast!" said MG.

Selah felt encouraged. This little pixie had just given her some good advice on how to handle the pain. It seemed to her that there was more to learn from MG.

Before Selah could ask her anything about being a fairy, MG came out with a golden-fringed scroll that she began to slowly unroll.

The letters S.T.U.B. were written in sparkling green glitter paint.

"Take a look at this," MG told Selah. "I want to share with you a great way to be in charge when you find yourself in difficult or scary situations. I want you to be able to feel the pain in life without letting it ruin your day. You'll remember this trick, because you'll never forget what it feels like to STUB your toe."

"OK," sighed Selah. "Would you agree that you got scared when you stubbed your toe?" asked MG.

"I sure was," said Selah. Holding up the scroll, MG proudly announced her magic plan.

Pointing to the sparkling green letters, she said. "This 'S' is for Stop. You have to stop...stop everything, even though you are feeling strong emotions and energy racing all throughout your body. The surprise of seeing me on the counter helped you stop feeling overwhelmed by the fear and pain you were experiencing.

"This 'T' is for Think. You think about what just happened. You actually figure out what is going on for you at the very moment you are upset. You notice the emotions you are experiencing and the sensations you feel in your body. Now that you have Stopped, let's Think. What was going on for you after you stubbed your toe?"

Selah paused for a moment and then said, "Well, I was surprised to see the chair, then I felt terrible pain in my toe. I felt angry and scared. Then I remembered that I was here by myself, and I felt even more scared. My toe was throbbing, and I began to think it might just fall right off!"

"Good thinking!" said MG. "OK, next, this 'U' is for Understand. Now that you have Stopped and Thought about what happened you begin to understand that your pinky toe is not broken, and that you will be fine. You can take a deep breath in order to figure out what is the best thing to do next."

Selah was getting the idea and piped up to finish MG's thought.

"So then the 'B' is for breathe, maybe?" guessed Selah.

"Exactly," said MG. "Taking a deep breath gives your mind and your body a chance to calm down. This helps you have some power over deciding what to do next."

As MG fully unrolled the scroll, she announced with a smile, "It looks like this, Selah!"

"STOP, THINK, UNDERSTAND, BREATHE!"

"S.T.U.B is a way for you to take care of yourself and make good choices when things are not going so well. Believe it or not, you already know how to take care of yourself. This plan just reminds you how to use the power you already have inside."

"Sugar Plums!" declared Selah (instead of saying words that would have gotten her in trouble with grown-ups). "This is all news to me. I didn't think I had any control over what I was feeling. Sometimes the feelings just come racing right through me."

"That's true, Selah. Sometimes you can't stop the energy of feelings, like feeling mad or frustrated, afraid or even feeling happy. But you can decide what you do with that energy. Feelings are natural, but what you do is up to *you*!" proclaimed MG.

"Let's use an example from something that happened today," suggested Morning Glory. Remember what happened today when your friend Sadie was talking with Aliya and the new girl came over and was making fun of them?" she asked.

Selah was amazed that MG knew about the terrible day she had in school. And, she was glad she could talk with someone about what had happened.

"Yeah," remembered Selah. "I was so mad that the back of my neck got all prickly, my stomach was in a knot, and I wanted to scream in her face because she was being so mean to my friends."

"That's true," declared MG. "She was being a bully, and she was picking on Sadie and Aliya by saying hurtful things to them. Now, think about what you did," said MG.

"I started yelling and screaming at her and was ready to fight when the teacher took us both into the school. It was not a pretty picture. We got in big trouble, and we even had to spend some time in the principal's office!" said Selah.

"Let's use the STUB plan and we'll rewind the scene and practice together how we might be able to handle the situation differently," said MG.

MG flew up about five inches from Selah's head and started spinning and singing. All of a sudden Selah was back in the school yard watching the scene from earlier in the day. She could see her friends and herself starting to fight with the new girl.

"Umm...what just happened?" Selah asked MG.

"We used the magic of the fifth dimension to rewind the day to take another look at what you could have done differently. Let's think about this together," directed MG.

"I see you watching this scene and it looks like even now you are getting upset. Let's Stop and take a step back and Think. What do you notice about the feelings in your body when you see your friends being yelled at?" asked the little pixie.

Selah thought for a moment. "Why, my stomach is hurting, and my heart is pounding in my chest and I feel really mad."

"Good noticing," smiled MG. "Your body is really your best friend, and it gives you wonderful information that you can use to make better decisions."

"Now that you have slowed down, can you feel anything different happening in your body?" MG asked.

"I feel a little better because the mess in my stomach is quiet, and my head is not pounding with anger. I think my heart is even slowing down."

"Exactly," said MG. "When you learn to stop and think, you have a better chance of making a good choice in any situation. Now let's Think some more about why the new kid might be threatening your friends this way so that we can Understand what is happening better."

"Well, she just moved here, and I guess she doesn't have any friends. She sure doesn't know how to make any either," said Selah.

"You are getting the hang of this," MG said with delight in her voice.

"If you understand that the new girl is feeling scared, how could you help?"

"Maybe I could make friends with her," suggested Selah.

"That's an amazing idea. How could you make friends with her and also help her see that what she is doing is hurting your friends? What ideas come to mind?"

"I could go right up to that new kid and tell her I don't like her talking to my friends if she is going to say mean things, because it just isn't a nice way to be in the world. I would tell her to stop it right now!" Selah said with some confidence in her voice.

"And then I could do something she would never expect. I could ask her where she was from and whether she would she like to have lunch with me and my friends."

"Selah, that is something grown-ups might not even think of doing. You are certainly ready to make a difference in that girl's life as well in your own life. Good for you."

"The next time a bully is mean to my friends, I'm going to Stop first before I just react," said Selah.

"Right," confirmed MG.

"Then, I am going to check in with my body and Think about what is really happening," said Selah.

"That will give you the information you need to Understand the situation. This way, you can make a better decision to help solve the problem, instead of making it worse for yourself or anyone else," directed MG.

"And if I remember to breathe, it will help make it all easier," smiled Selah.

"That's true," said MG. "You can always use your breath to help make things easier. Your breath is like a best friend who is with you all the time, kind of like I am." MG's eyes twinkled as she smiled at Selah.

Selah was excited to try using STUB again and even more thrilled that she could share her pink cupcake with MG. She had had almost forgotten that her little pinky toe had been hurting.

The End

Discussion Questions for you to think about and share with others, especially children.

Hurts come in many forms: a hurt body, hurt feelings, a hurting heart, or hurting words. Many times our bodies feel the pain and confusion even before we realize what is happening.

1. When you get hurt, why might you need to just Stop before you do anything else?

2. Selah noticed some interesting things happening to her body when she got hurt. Do you remember any times when you got hurt (physically or emotionally) and felt something change in your body such as a stomach ache, a pounding heart, or even a "prickly" neck?

3. If you Stop and Think after you get hurt in any way, how might this help you make a better choice about what you should do next?

4. Can you think of a time when you got hurt, and then acted in a way that caused trouble for you or made the situation much worse?

5. What does it mean to have choices when it comes to the way you behave and what do you think it means to make healthy and thoughtful choices?

Note to Parents and Caregivers

Often we watch our children flail out of control because of emotional upset and misunderstood feelings. The energy of strong emotions seems to take over as if it were a magical spell, confusing and astounding child and adult alike. Because children don't yet have a good understanding of their emotions and how to deal with them, they are more easily overwhelmed by the feelings. This causes unnecessary upset and suffering, and sometimes escalates a situation to hysteria.

STUB is a technique and a skill that can help children and the adults who love them better understand any given situation in their lives and then make better choices. By helping children know their own resources and their innate abilities to navigate through difficult situations, we can help to give them more control and ultimately the power to make thoughtful and helpful choices.

Help your child learn to Stop by modeling and practicing the actual act of stopping the behaviors that are fueled by the feelings and emotions. Those behaviors might include such things as yelling, screaming, crying, using hurt-ful, angry words and statements, and even violent threats. There might even be a flood of negative thoughts that take over and keep the hurt going. You can model for your chil-dren by demonstrating that you can actually say "Stop" to yourself before you go on to the next step.

Help your child start to Think about their body as a valuable instrument of information. The body has a know-ing that we do not tap into and only by modeling and in-struction can children understand the value of noticing the sensations in their bodies.

When we Understand what is happening, choice be-comes an option and inner wisdom and knowing is availa-ble.

Breathing is a natural function of being a human. Help children come to know their breath as a very special friend whom they can call upon at any time. The breath is the champion of living in harmony with yourself and others throughout life.

Resources to Inspire

10% Happier, by Dan Harris

Alcoholics Anonymous

A Burning Desire, by Kevin Griffin

Better Than Before, by Gretchen Rubin

Breaking the Habit of Being Yourself: How to Lose Your
Mind and Create a New One, by Joe Dispenza

Creative Visualization, by Shakti Gawain

Daring Greatly, by Brene Brown

E-Squared: Nine Do-It-Yourself Energy Experiments that
Prove Your Thoughts Create Your Reality, by Pam Grout

Facing Love Addictions, by Pia Melody

Healing the Addicted Brain, by Harold Urschel

Is It Love or Is It Addiction? by Brenda Schaeffer

Jumping on Water by Ted Karam

Living in the Light by Shakti Gawain

Living Sober Sucks (but living drunk sucks more),
by Mark Tuschel

Mindfulness Based Relapse Prevention, by Sarah Bowen,
Neha Chawla, and Alan Marlott

Mindfulness for Beginners: Reclaiming the Present Moment
and Your Life, by Jon Kabat-Zinn

Radical Acceptance, by Tara Brach

Recover! Stop Acting Like an Addict! by Stanton Peel

ReWired: A Bold New Approach to Addiction and Recovery, by Erica Spiegelman

Rising Strong, by Brene Brown

The 7 Habits of Highly Effective Teenagers, by Sean Covey

The Gifts of Imperfection, by Brene Brown

The Heart of Addiction, by Lance Dodes

The Honeymoon Effect, the Science of Creating Heaven on Earth, by Bruce Lipton

The Miracle of Mindfulness: An Introduction to the Practice of Meditation, by Thich Nhat Hanh

The Miracle of the Breath, by Andy Caponigro

The Power of Habit: Why We Do What We Do in Life and Business, by Charles Duhigg

The Secret Code of Success, by Noah St. John Self- Compassion, by Kristin Neff

The Slight Edge, by Jeff Olson

The Tapping Solution, by Nick Ortner

The Whole Brain Child, by Dan Siegle

The Will Power Instinct, by Kelly McGonigal

Think and Grow Rich, by Napoleon Hill

About the Author

Gena Rotas, LICSW, MSW, M.Ed. is a professional speaker and trainer, with a private psychotherapy and coaching practice where she supports the efforts of women, children, and families to come to know themselves better, and practice  self-care and self-love. She teaches the skills and strategies of mindfulness through what she calls "Mindful and Compassionate Coaching." With her passion for helping those with addictions, she uses the Mindfulness Based Relapse Prevention Program, which has been instrumental throughout her work. She also completed a year-long certification program for Mindful Schools. The combination of education and social work has given Gena an important advantage in teaching the skills that can profoundly help people change, flourish, and thrive in life.

One of Gena's core beliefs is that happiness is a choice, which supports the idea that what we need to do is have the awareness, desire, courage, and passion to create joy in our lives. Her enduring message affirms that when we find peace, purpose, and enthusiasm within our own hearts, we can change the world for the better.

She traveled the country working for Performance Learning Systems training teachers in the how-to skills of classroom management and positive relationships with students. She taught for many years as an adjunct instructor of graduate level programs and was a psychotherapist with prisoners, victims of trauma and abuse, and those in recovery from addictions. Her influence as an adjustment counselor in an inner city middle school allowed her the opportunity to coach children, teachers, parents, and community leaders towards harmony and productive relationships. Through the years she has provided teacher training and staff development programs for Massachusetts and Connecticut School Districts. Her ability to meet the needs of corporate and business training has been delivered to such organizations as MassMutual Financial and Bay State Medical Center. She has also applied the mindfulness concepts and counselor training she developed to a chain of weight loss centers in and around a number of New England cities.

In 2006, Gena self-published her first book, *Love Your Slim Self*, a guide to loving yourself first in order to reach your desired health and well-being, which she has used in her private practice to help her patients sustain weight loss using her "slim from within" model.

Gena holds a BA from Western Connecticut State University, an MA from Fairfield University, and an MSW from the University of Connecticut. She is a Licensed Independent Clinical Social Worker, a Practitioner in Emotional Freedom Technique (EFT) or Tapping, HeartMath, and Mindfulness. She is active in ProSpeakers (an advanced Toastmasters club) and the Women Business Owners Alliance.

Take Your Next Step with Gena

Gena Rotas will mindfully orchestrate, design, and deliver a road map that will get you to where you want to go.

School Systems, business and industry, nonprofit organizations, community groups, children, parents, and individuals have all benefited by her expertise.

Gena understands that information sticks when people are engaged and having fun. She will customize her delivery in both length and content for your group when she presents a training, workshop or motivational talk. Her skill-based presentations teach usable strategies participants can implement immediately to improve their lives.

For groups that find Gena's passionate message and powerful techniques helpful and want more extensive training, Gena customizes training programs that not only teach mindfulness skills, but help participates integrate the principles of healthy decision-making and self-care into their daily lives.

Mindfulness Training in the Classroom
Gena is certified to deliver the Mindfulness Curriculum to children from Kindergarten through twelfth grade. The skills she teaches help children enhance their executive functioning in order to focus their attention better. The Mindfulness skills teach children to regulate their emotional landscape by taking the fear out of anxiety, so they can

feel braver, calmer, and learn easier. Learning Mindfulness has demonstrated profound ability to increase the awareness of compassion and empathy for oneself and for others. For many, these skills are life changing. Teachers learn from these exercises so they can continue to reinforce the skills once Gena completes the curriculum.

Personal Coaching (in person, by phone, or by Skype)

For those who want an individualize program and the personal accountability of working one-on-one, Gena offers private consulting and coaching to support your efforts to thrive and flourish in life.

Made in United States
North Haven, CT
03 May 2023

36199226R00124